Country Farm Scenes
Color By Number For Adults
Nature, Animal and Easy Designs
Adult Coloring Book

By Color Questopia

Thank you for your purchase!

Claim your FREE digital copy of our Highlight Reel Color By Number Book:

Check out our website: colorquestopia.com

Join our Facebook group: facebook.com/colorquestopia

Follow us on Instagram: @colorquestopia

Did you enjoy this book? Please leave us a review!

https://geni.us/cqreview

Color By Number Tips

1. **Relax and have fun**
   Let your cares slip away as you color the images. Take your time. Coloring is a meditative activity and there's no wrong way to do it. Feel free to color as you listen to music, watch TV, lounge in bed- do whatever relaxes you most! You can also color while you're out and about- on the train or at a cafe- take the book with you anywhere you go. Coloring is therapeutic and is great for stress relief and relaxation!

2. **Colors corresponding to each number are shown on the back cover of the book**
   Each number corresponds to a color shown on the back of the book. You can match the color as closely as you like- but feel free to change the color or the shade if you don't have the exact color match- that's totally fine. Although this is a color by number book, it's completely okay to get creative and color the images with whichever colors you like and have. The numbers are there to be a guide and to allow you to color without having to focus your energy on choosing colors.

3. **Choose your coloring tools**
   Everyone has their favorite coloring markers, crayons, pencils, pens- even paints! Feel free to color with any tool that you like! If you choose markers or paints, we recommend putting a blank sheet of paper or cardboard behind each image, so that your colors don't run onto the next image.

   Enjoy!

1. Light Brown
2. Brown
3. Medium Brown
4. Dark Brown
5. Yellow
6. Dark Green
7. Green
8. Light Green
9. Neon Green
10. Medium Green
11. Gray
12. Light Gray
13. Soft Violet
14. Blue
15. Navy Blue
16. Sky Blue
17. Light Pink

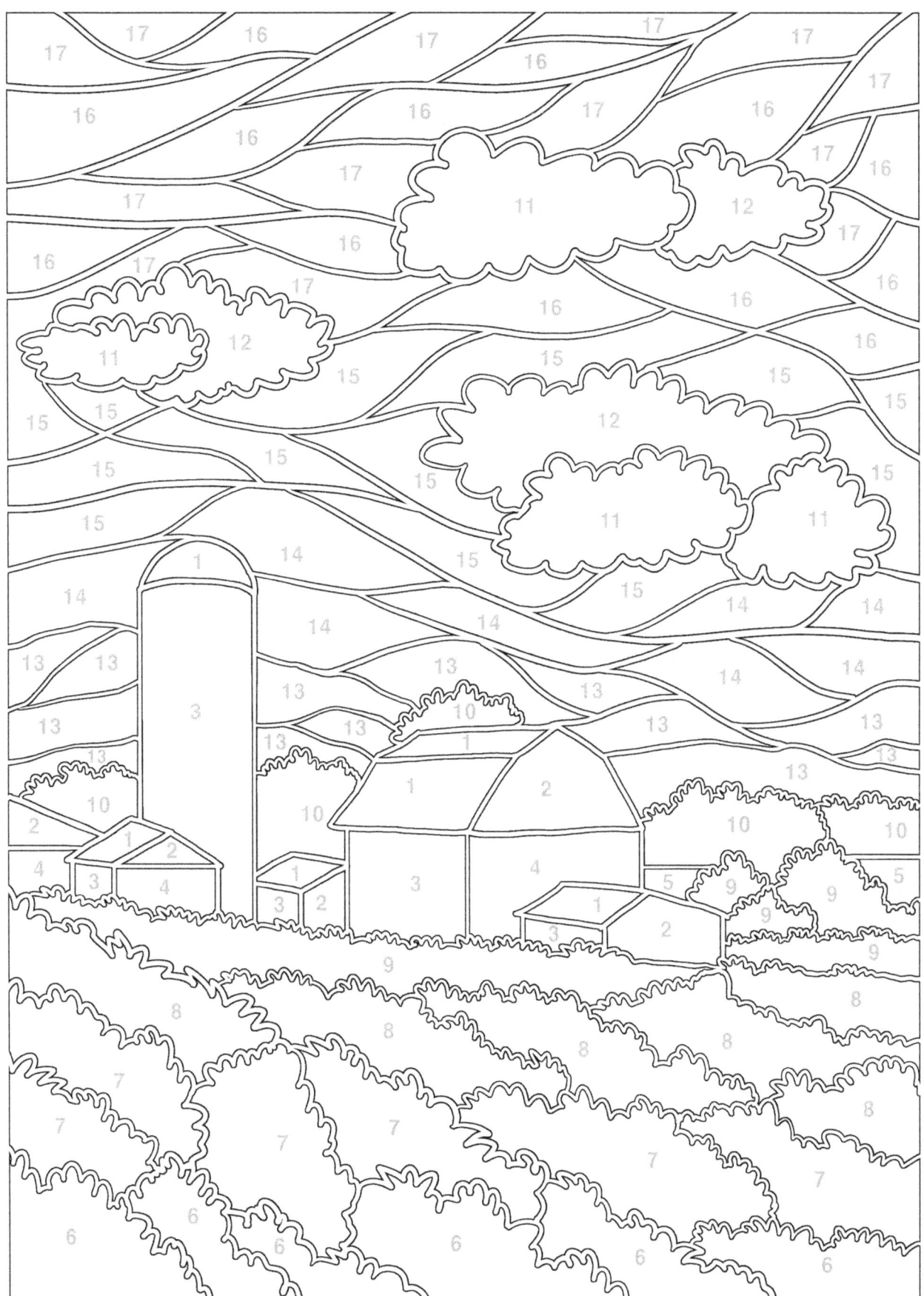

1. Brown
2. Medium Brown
3. Light Brown
4. Dark Brown
5. Yellow
6. Light Green
7. Dark Orange
8. Dark Red
9. Dark Green
10. Medium Green
11. Green
12. Neon Green
13. Blue
14. Light Pink
15. Navy Blue
16. Sky Blue
17. Soft Violet

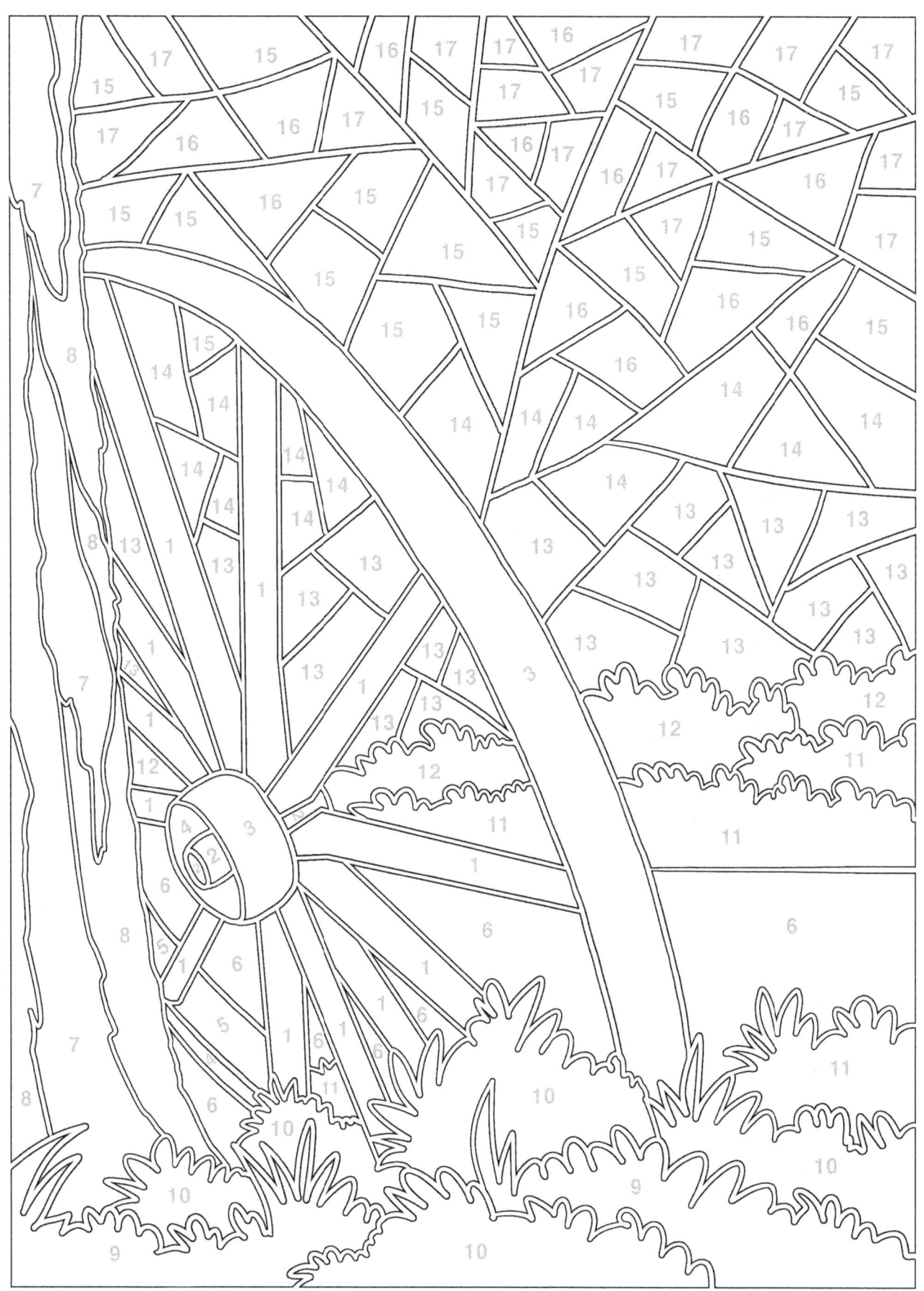

1. Orange

2. Dark Orange

3. Brown

4. Dark Yellow

5. Yellow

6. Red

7. Dark Red

8. Light Green

9. Dark Brown

10. Medium Brown

11. Dark Green

12. Green

13. Neon Green

14. Army Green

15. Light Brown

16. Blue

17. Sky Blue

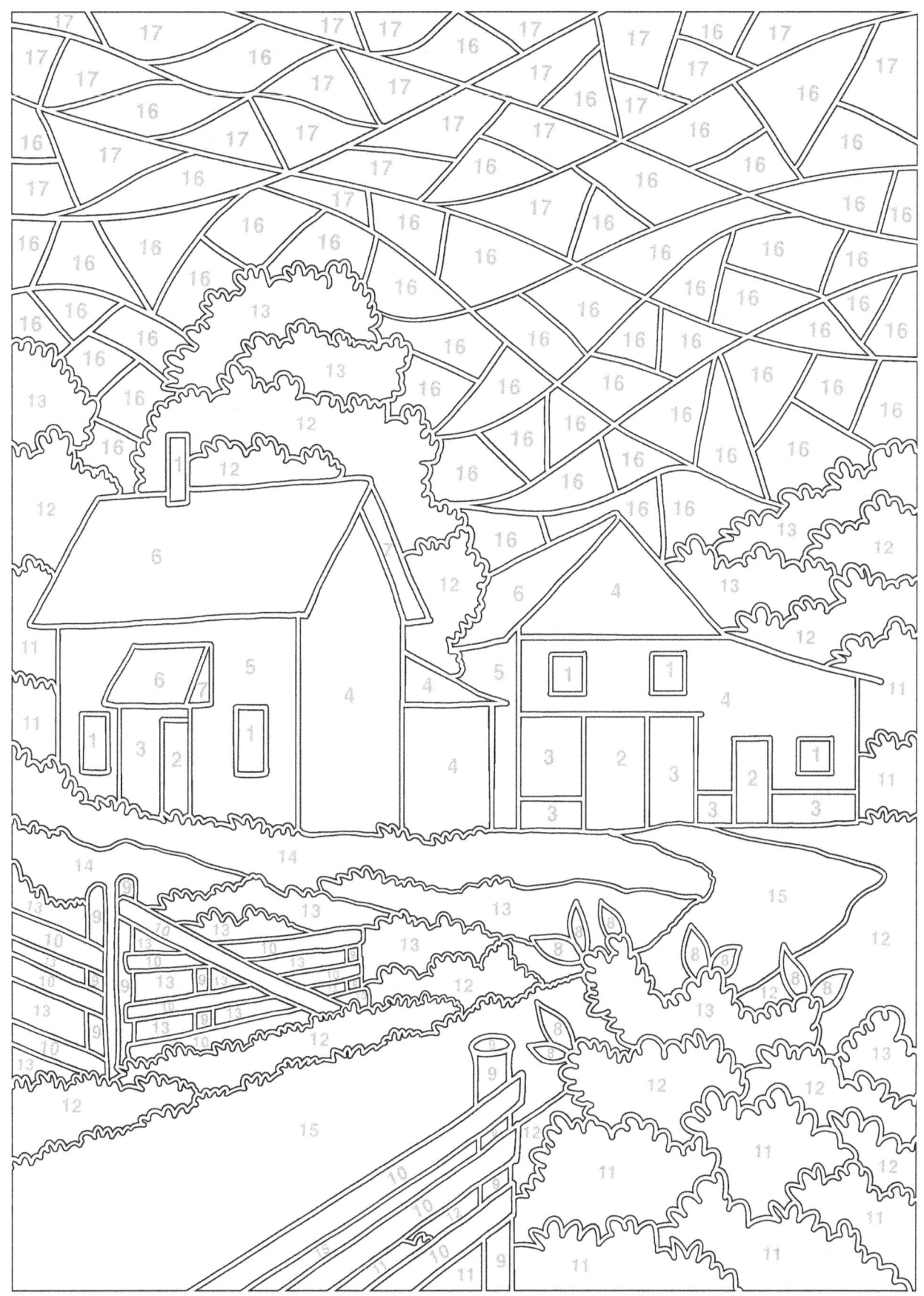

1. Dark Brown

2. Dark Red

3. Light Brown

4. Medium Brown

5. Dark Brown

6. Navy Blue

7. Sky Blue

8. Soft Violet

9. Orange

10. Light Gray

11. Gray

12. Yellow

13. Neon Green

14. Dark Orange

15. Red

16. Green

17. Light Green

18. Brown

19. Blue

20. Light Blue

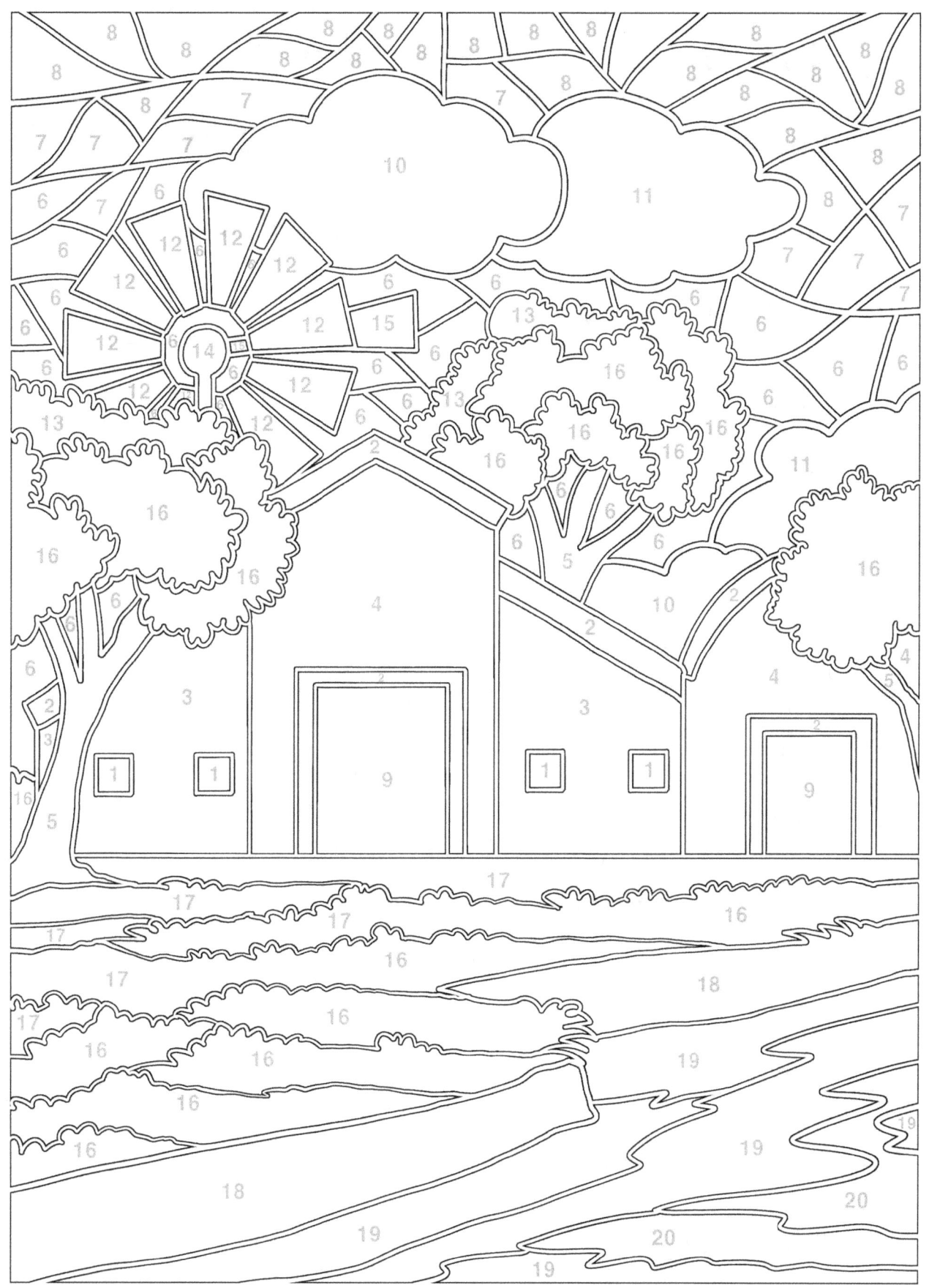

1. Dark Orange

2. Yellow

3. Red

4. Medium Brown

5. Light Gray

6. Orange

7. Dark Green

8. Medium Green

9. Light Brown

10. Brown

11. Light Orange

12. Army Green

13. Light Green

14. Neon Green

15. Dark Brown

16. Gray

17. Light Gray

18. Sky Blue

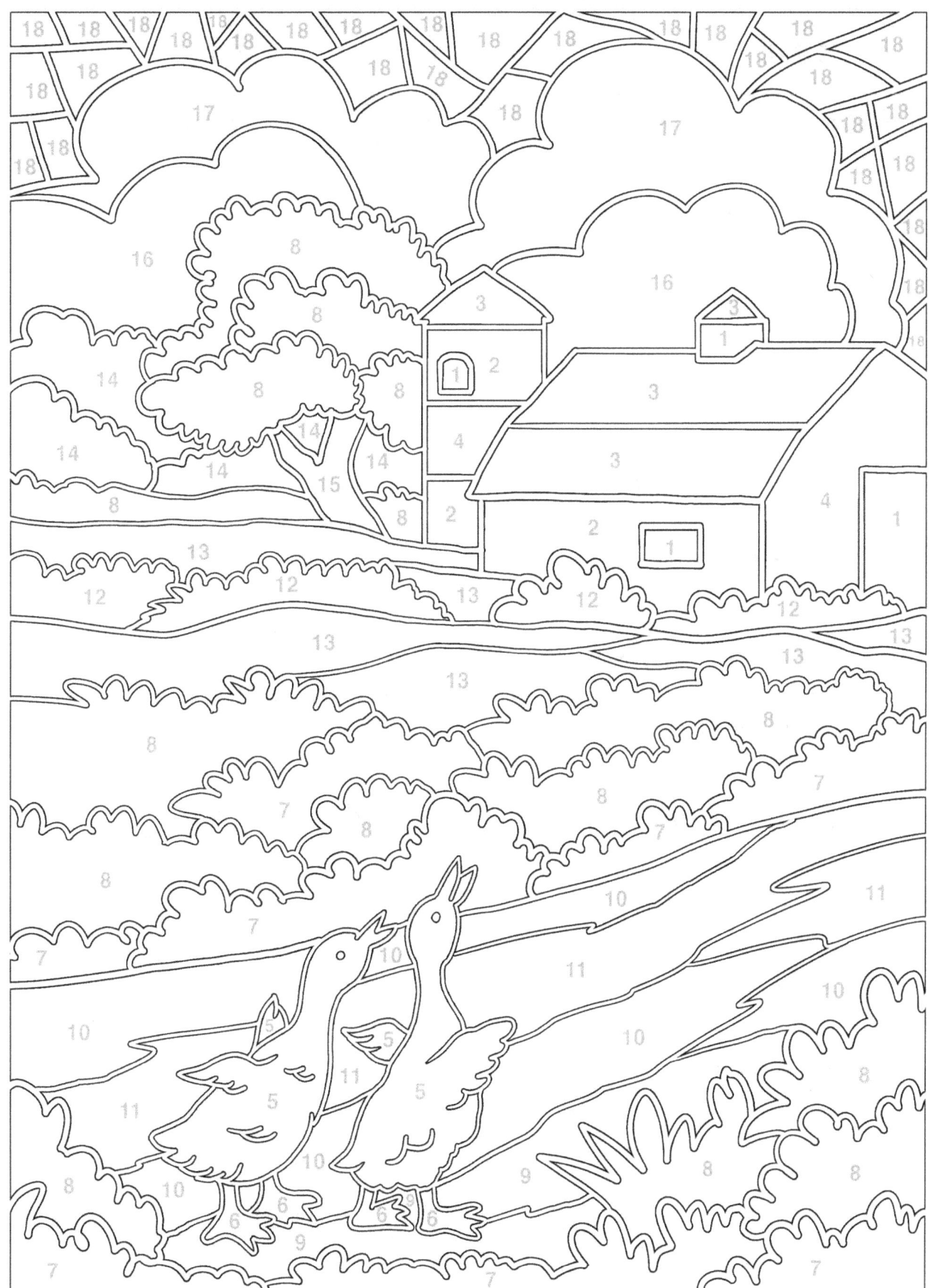

1. Black

2. Pink

3. Dark Brown

4. Brown

5. Medium Brown

6. Dark Green

7. Green

8. Medium Green

9. Light Green

10. Light Brown

11. Light Orange

12. Neon Green

13. Army Green

14. Blue

15. Baby blue

16. Navy Blue

17. Light Blue

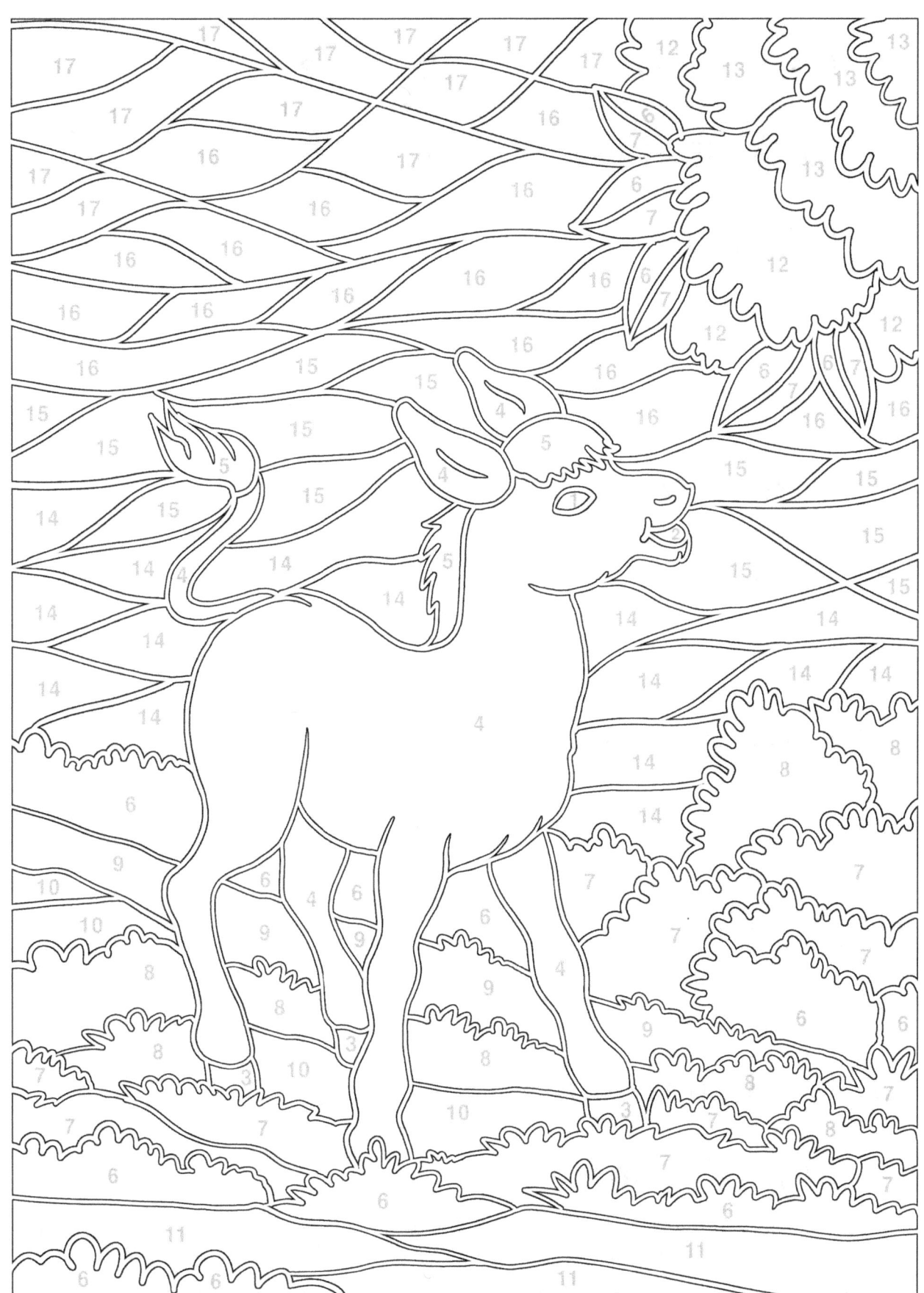

1. Dark Brown
2. Dark Orange
3. Orange
4. Red
5. Dark Red
6. Soft Violet
7. Violet
8. Yellow
9. Light Brown
10. Brown
11. Dark Green
12. Green
13. Medium Green
14. Light Green
15. Neon Green
16. Blue
17. Light Blue

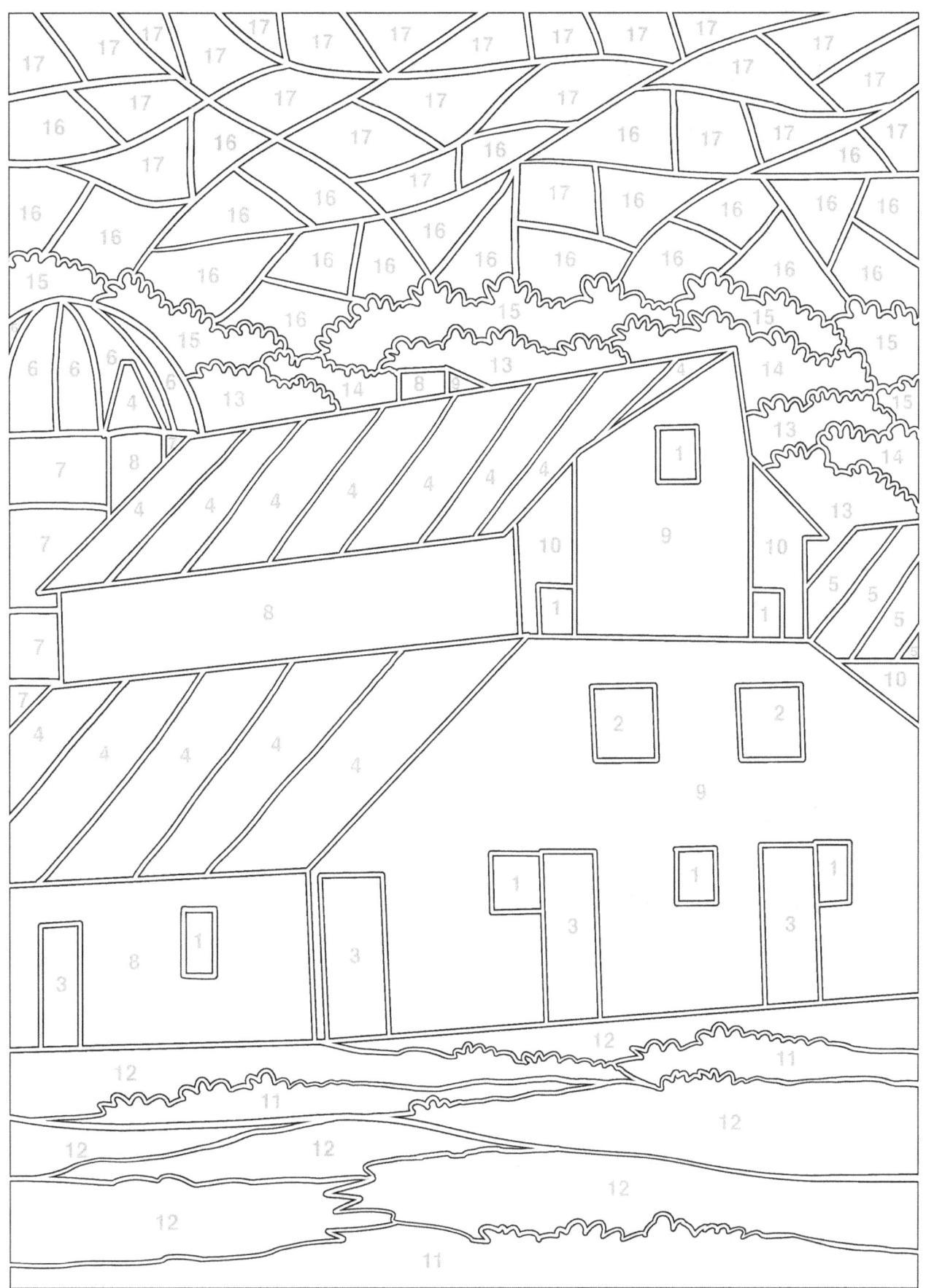

1. Dark Brown
2. Yellow
3. Orange
4. Light Orange
5. Light Red
6. Red
7. Brown
8. Dark Green
9. Green
10. Neon Green
11. Light Green
12. Green
13. Army Green
14. Light Brown
15. Light Yellow
16. Blue
17. Light Blue

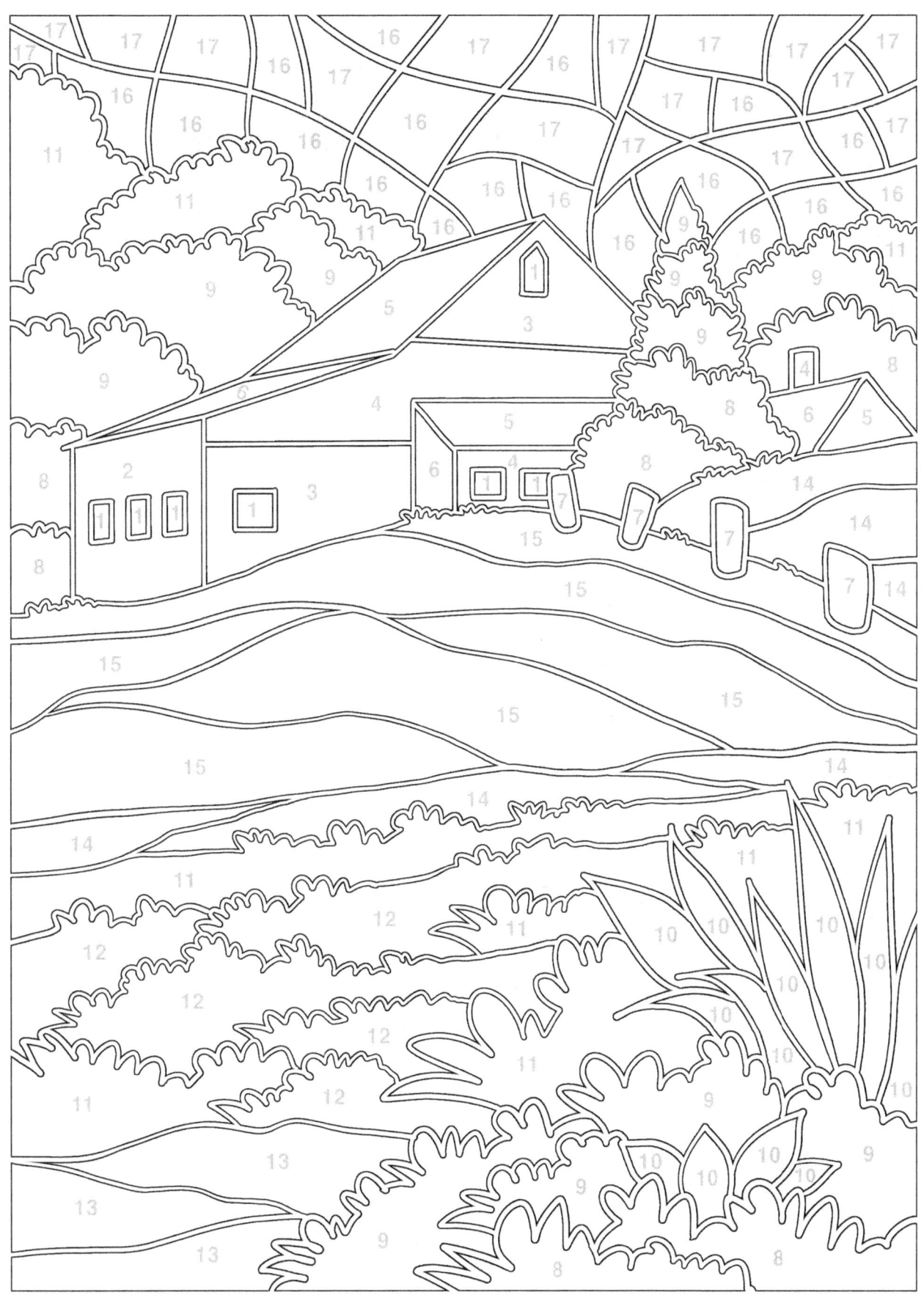

1. Black

2. Dark Brown

3. Pink

4. Brown

5. Light Pink

6. Light Brown

7. Dark Green

8. Medium Green

9. Green

10. Light Green

11. Dark Green

12. Neon Green

13. Army Green

14. Gray

15. Light Gray

16. Blue

17. Light Blue

18. Navy Blue

19. Baby blue

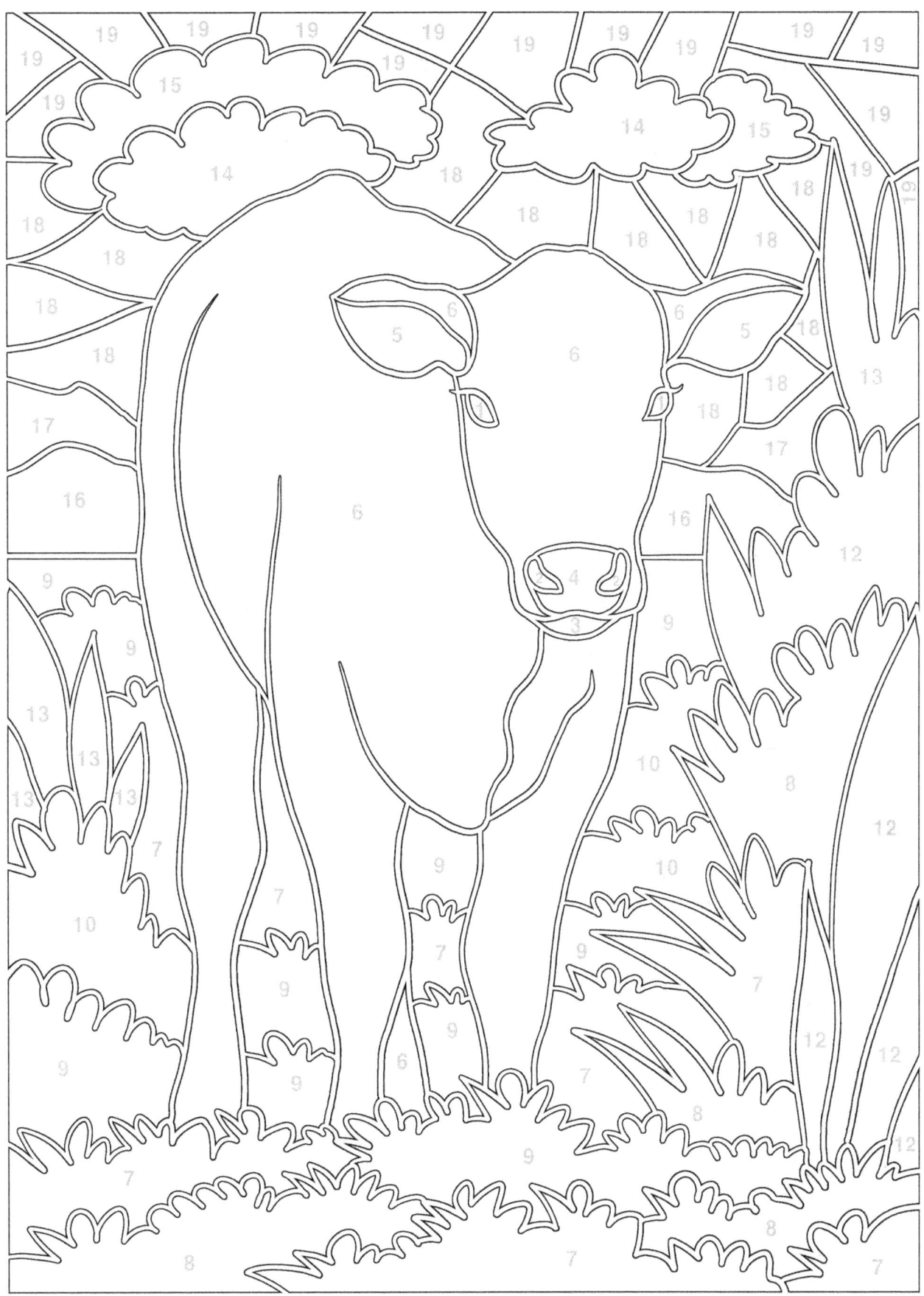

1. Light Yellow

2. Light Red

3. Orange

4. Yellow

5. Brown

6. Light Orange

7. Red

8. Light Purple

9. Dark Orange

10. Medium Purple

11. Light Brown

12. Dark Brown

13. Dark Green

14. Green

15. Light Green

16. Blue

17. Light Blue

18. Baby Blue

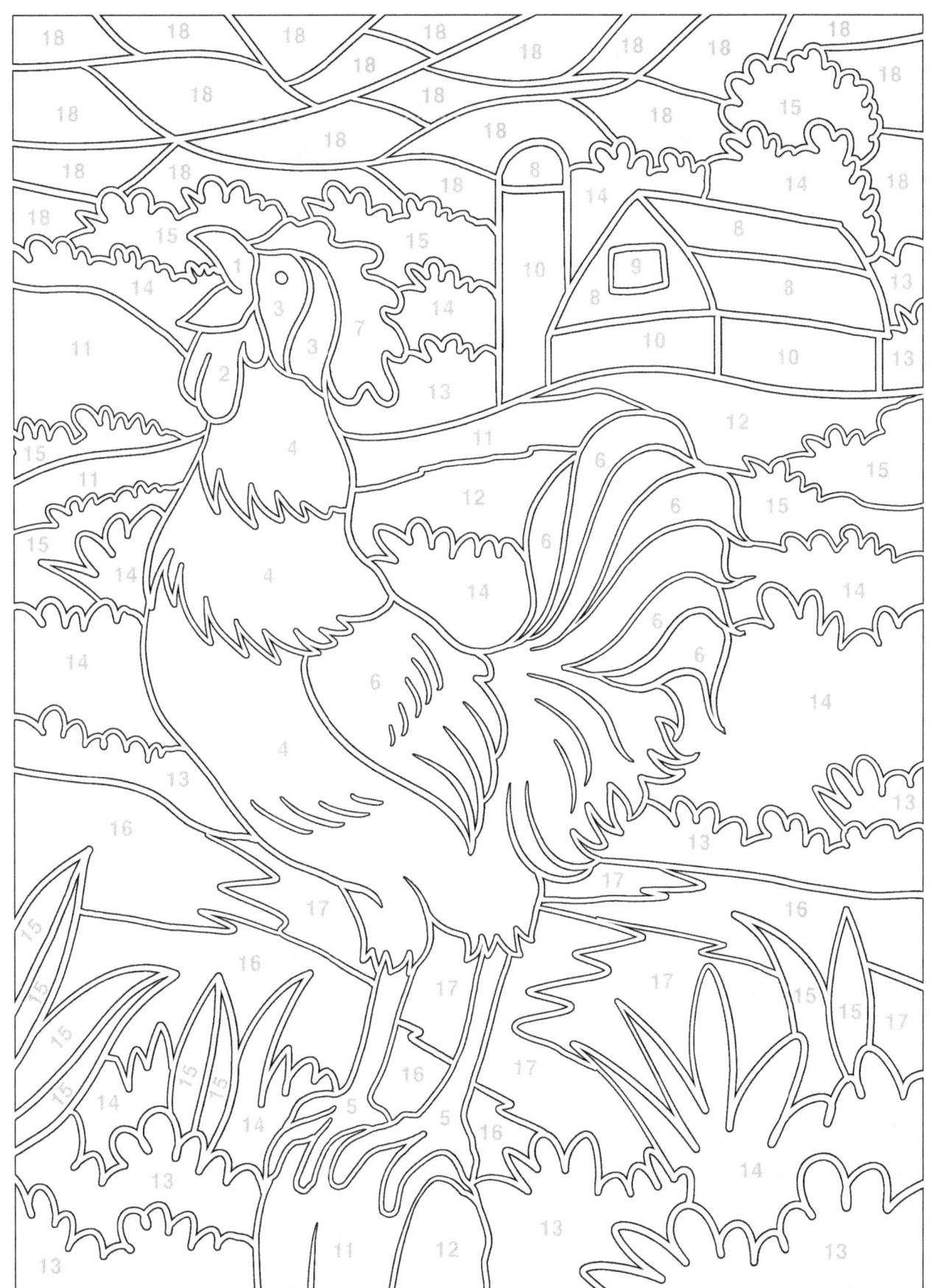

1. Dark Brown

2. Light Brown

3. Soft Violet

4. Yellow

5. Orange

6. Violet

7. Red

8. Brown

9. Dark Green

10. Light Green

11. Neon Green

12. Army Green

13. Medium Green

14. Blue

15. Light Blue

16. Navy Blue

17. Baby blue

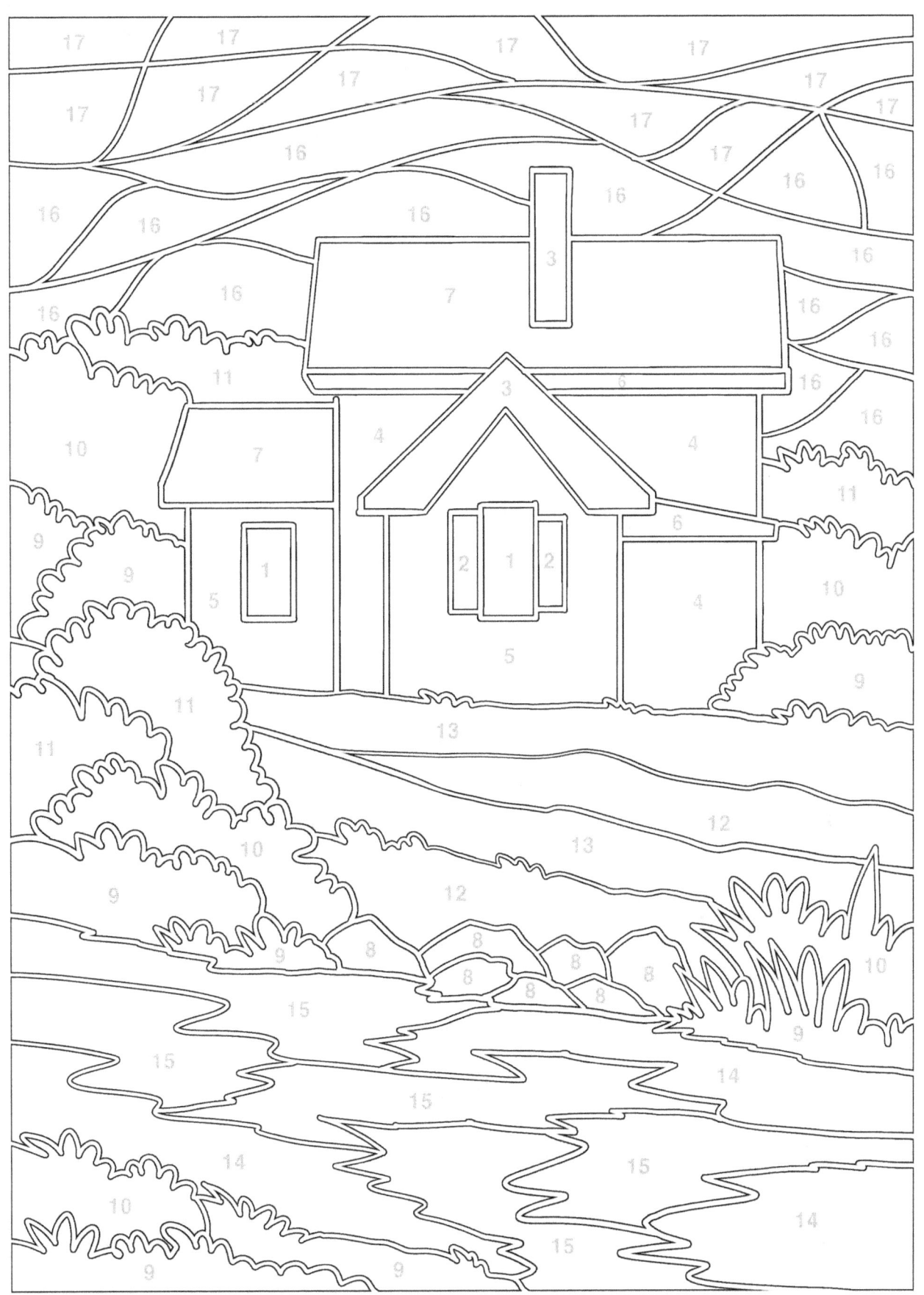

1. Black

2. Dark Brown

3. Light Pink

4. Dark Yellow

5. Brown

6. Green

7. Dark Green

8. Medium Green

9. Army Green

10. Neon Green

11. Light Green

12. Gray

13. Medium Gray

14. Light Gray

15. Blue

16. Navy Blue

17. Light Blue

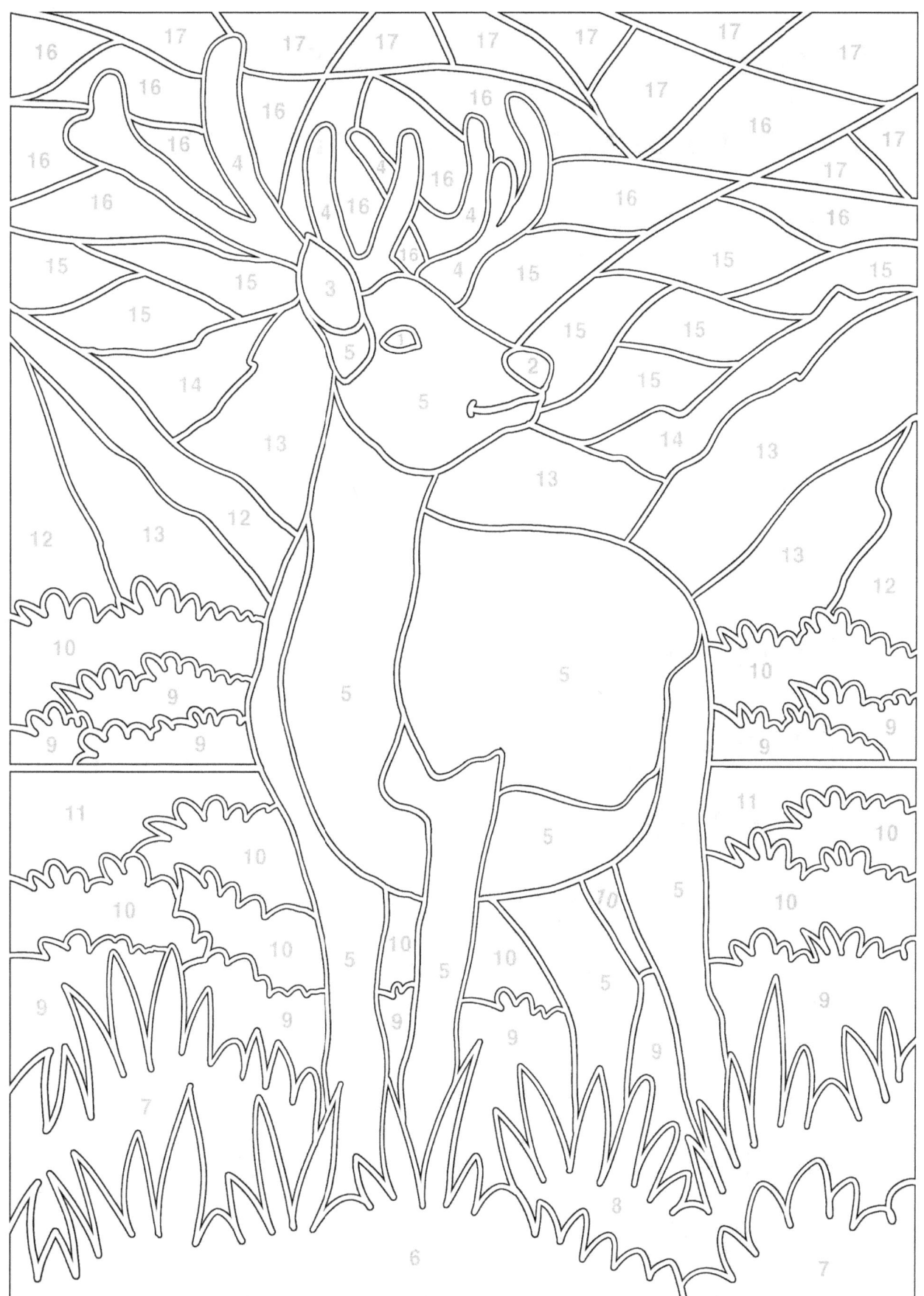

1. Brown

2. Medium Brown

3. Dark Yellow

4. Light Brown

5. Yellow

6. Light Green

7. Green

8. Neon Green

9. Army Green

10. Light Yellow

11. Medium Green

12. Dark Green

13. Light Gray

14. Medium Gray

15. Dark Gray

16. Blue

17. Light Blue

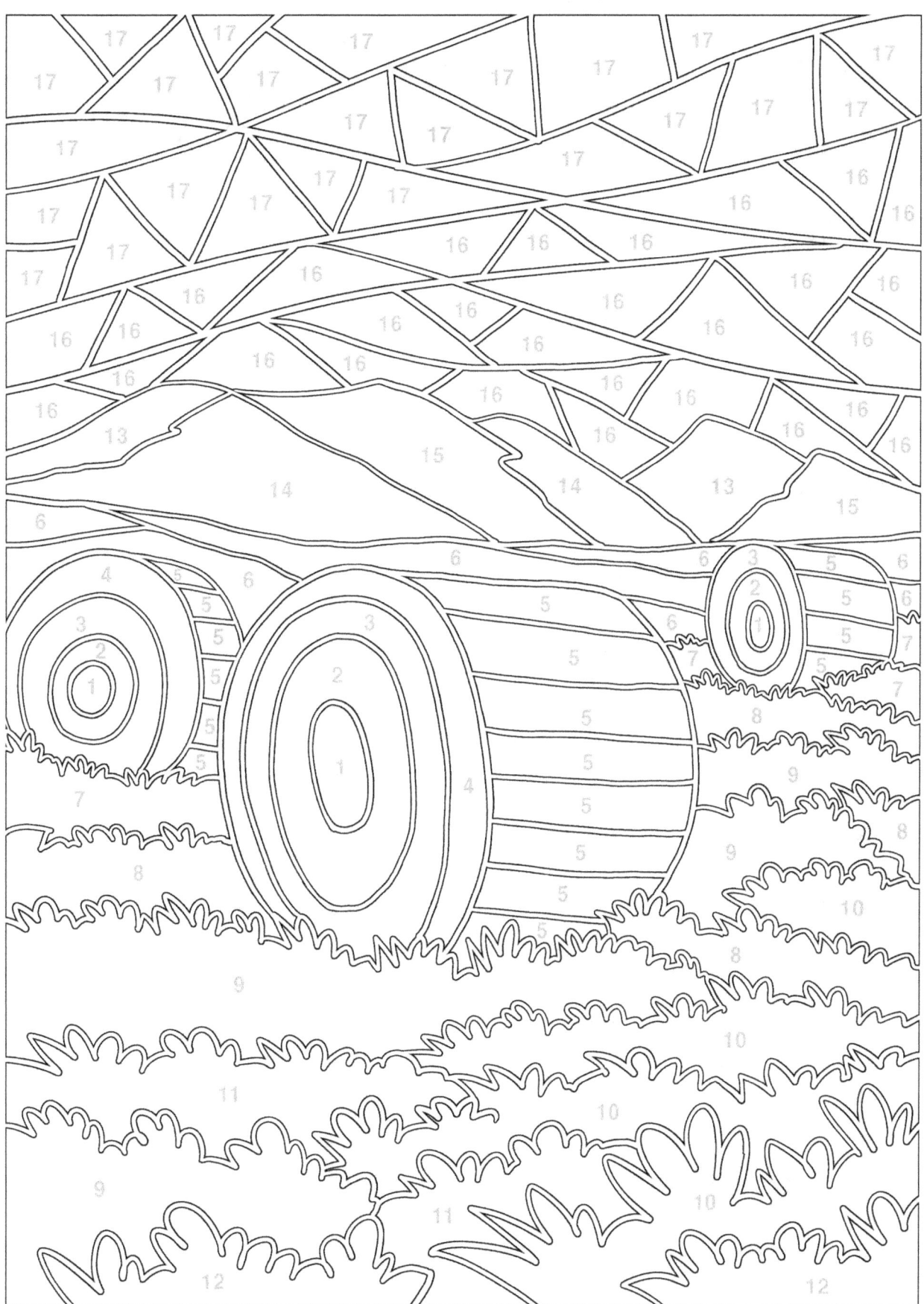

1. Black

2. Dark Brown

3. Light Brown

4. Medium Brown

5. Brown

6. Dark Yellow

7. Light Green

8. Army Green

9. Green

10. Medium Green

11. Neon Green

12. Gray

13. Medium Gray

14. Light Gray

15. Soft Violet

16. Blue

17. Light Blue

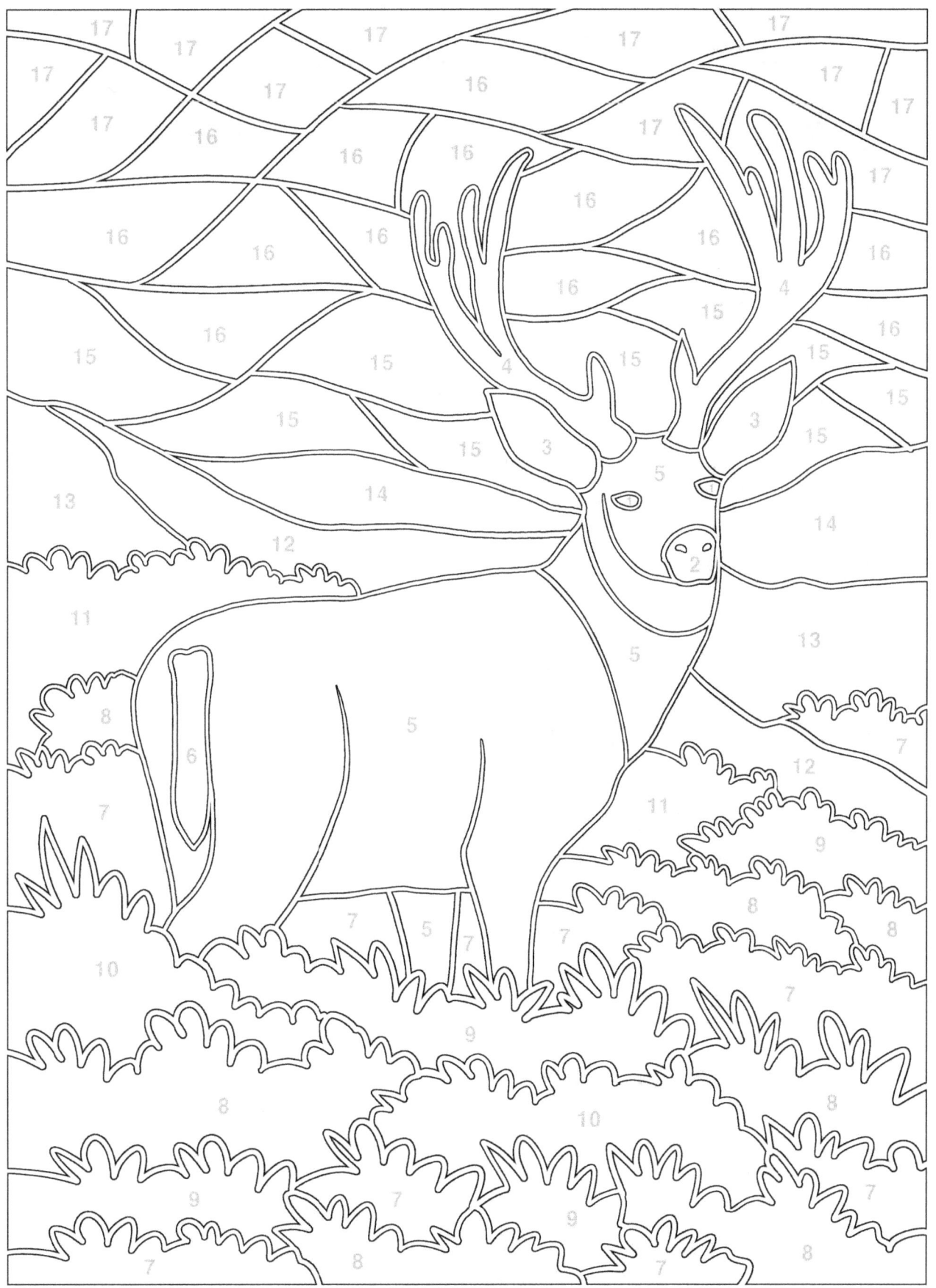

1. Yellow

2. Red

3. Light Brown

4. Orange

5. Medium Blue

6. Navy Blue

7. Brown

8. Dark Green

9. Medium Green

10. Neon Green

11. Light Green

12. Green

13. Medium Brown

14. Brown

15. Light Blue

16. Blue

17. Soft Violet

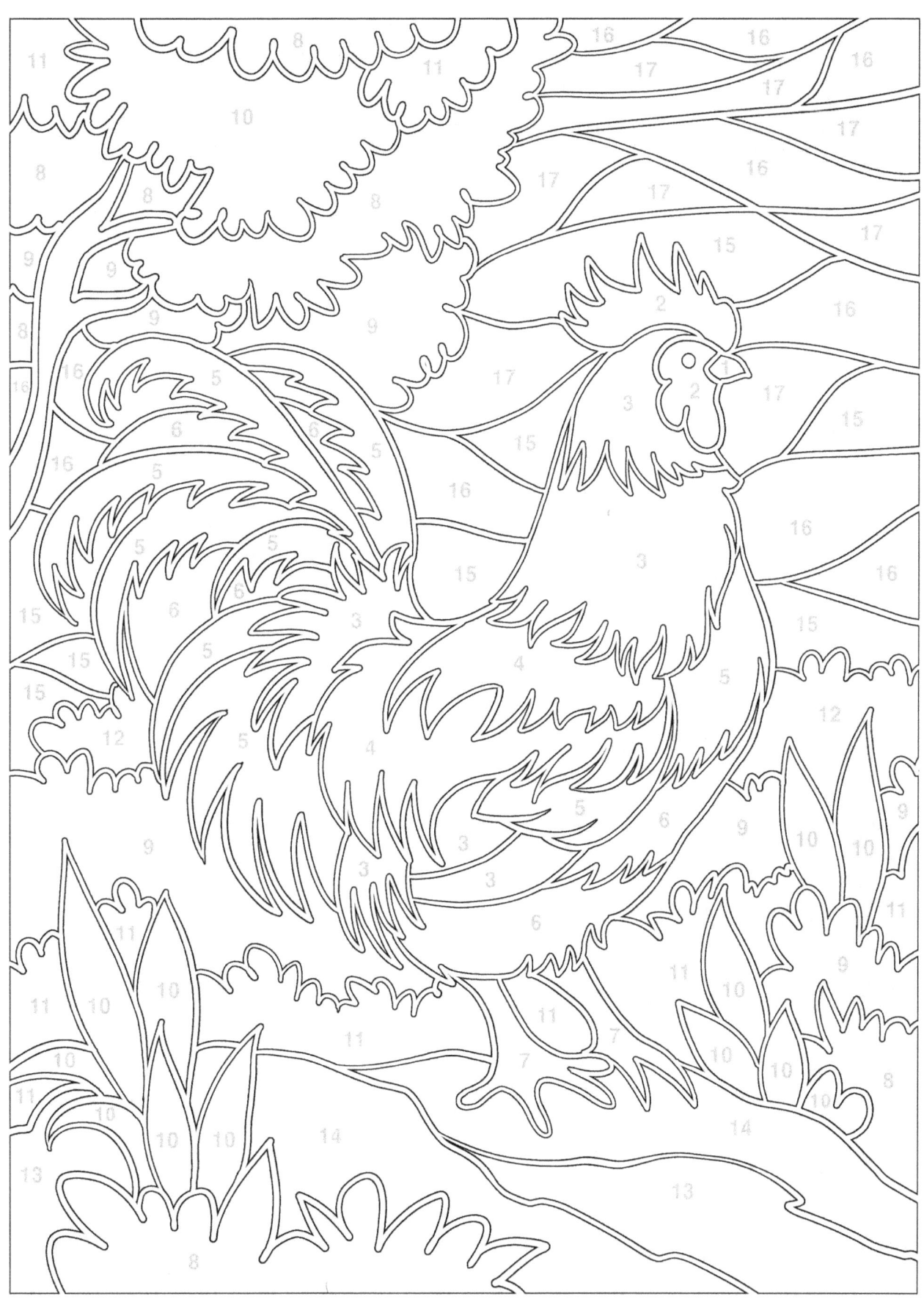

1. Red

2. Dark Red

3. Pink

4. Dark Brown

5. Red

6. Yellow

7. Dark Green

8. Medium Green

9. Army Green

10. Green

11. Light Green

12. Light Brown

13. Brown

14. Gray

15. Light Gray

16. Blue

17. Light Blue

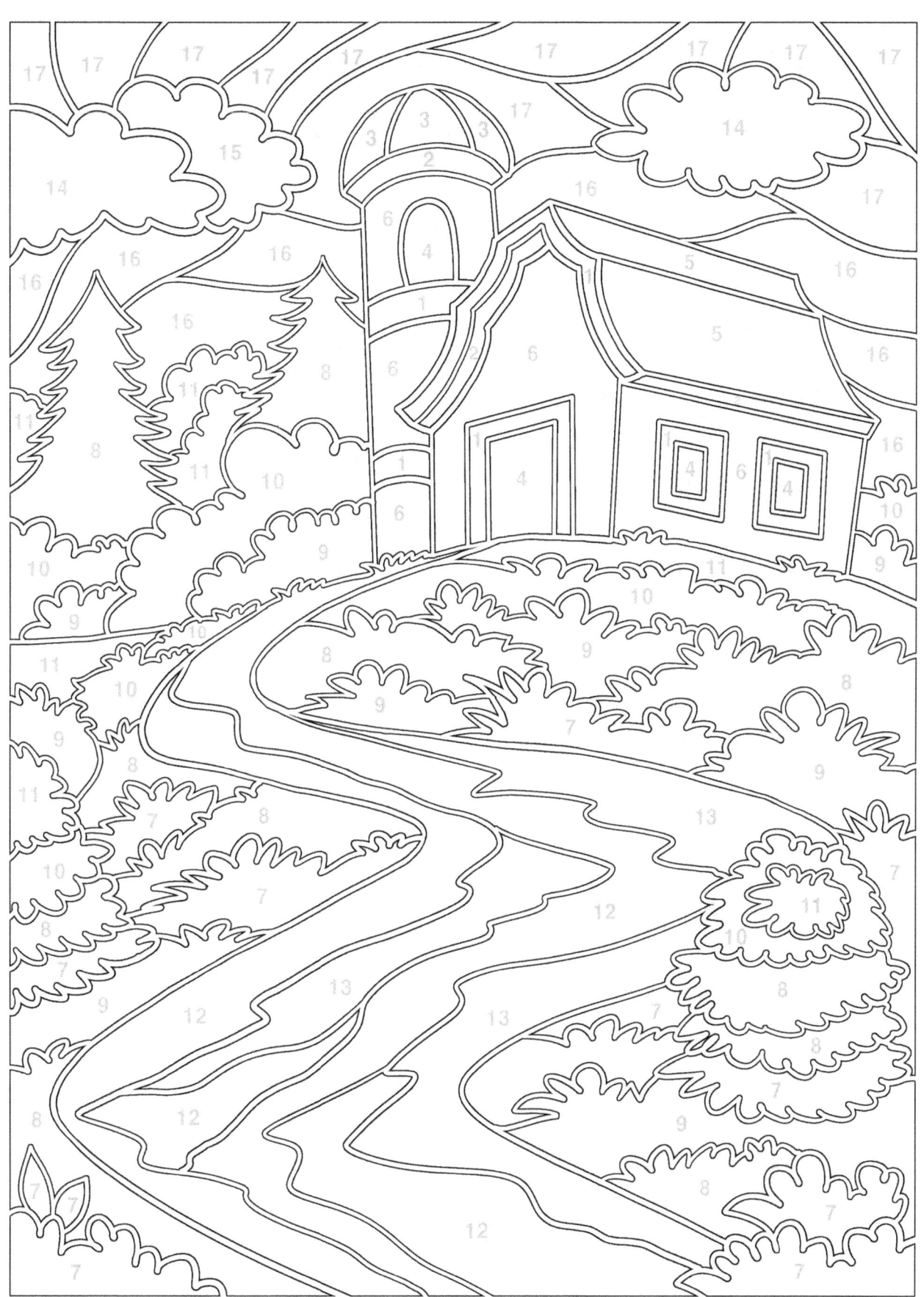

1. Yellow
2. Red
3. Light Yellow
4. Orange
5. Dark Orange
6. Medium blue
7. Navy Blue
8. Light Brown
9. Green
10. Light Green
11. Neon Green
12. Medium Purple
13. Light Purple
14. Medium Gray
15. Gray
16. Light Gray
17. Light Blue

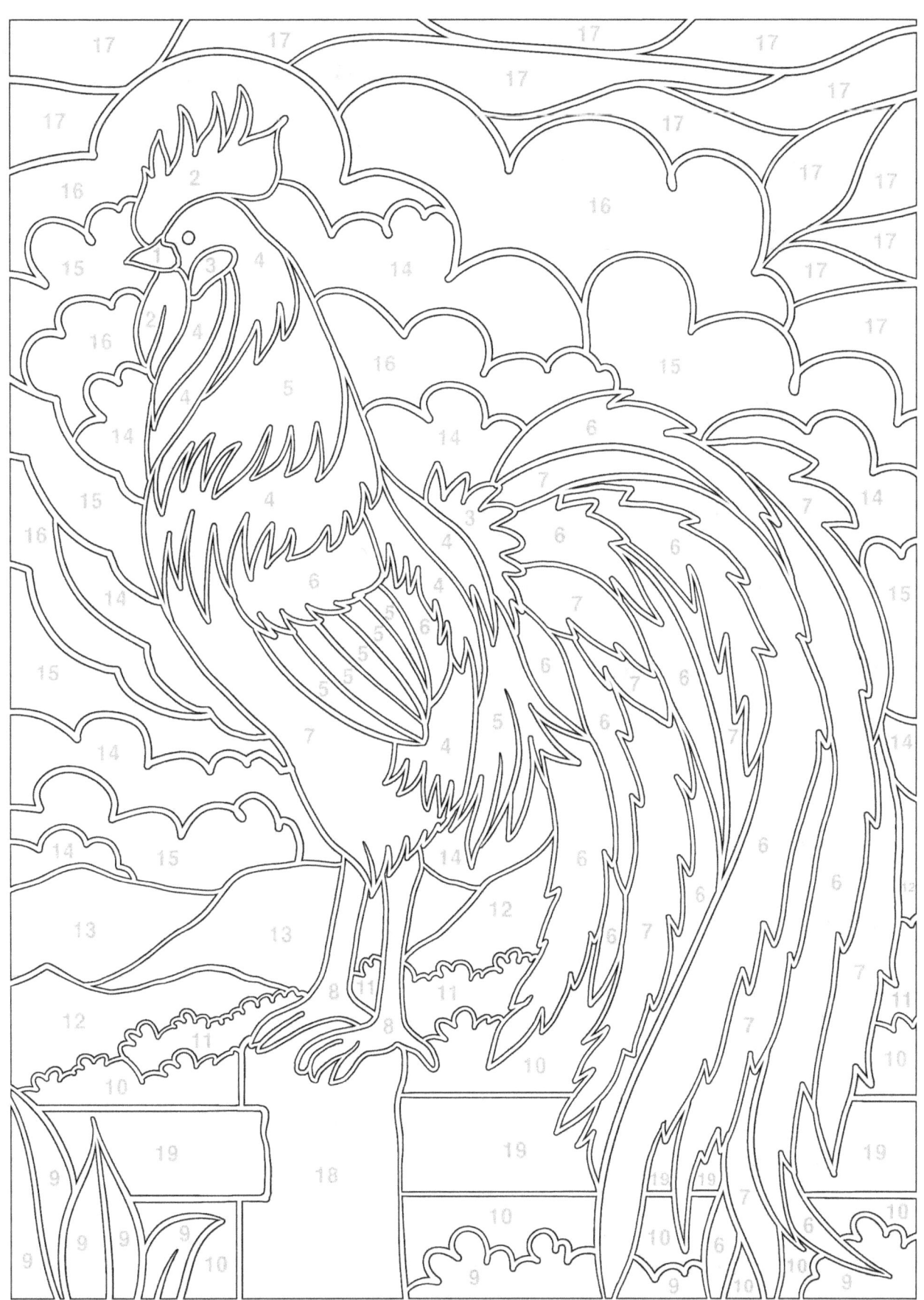

1. Black

2. Reddish Brown

3. Dark Brown

4. Light Brown

5. Golden Yellow

6. Orange

7. Red

8. Dark Yellow

9. Light Yellow

10. Beige

11. Sky Blue

12. Medium Blue

13. Light Green

14. Medium Green

15. Dark Green

16. Light pink

17. Pink

18. Royal Blue

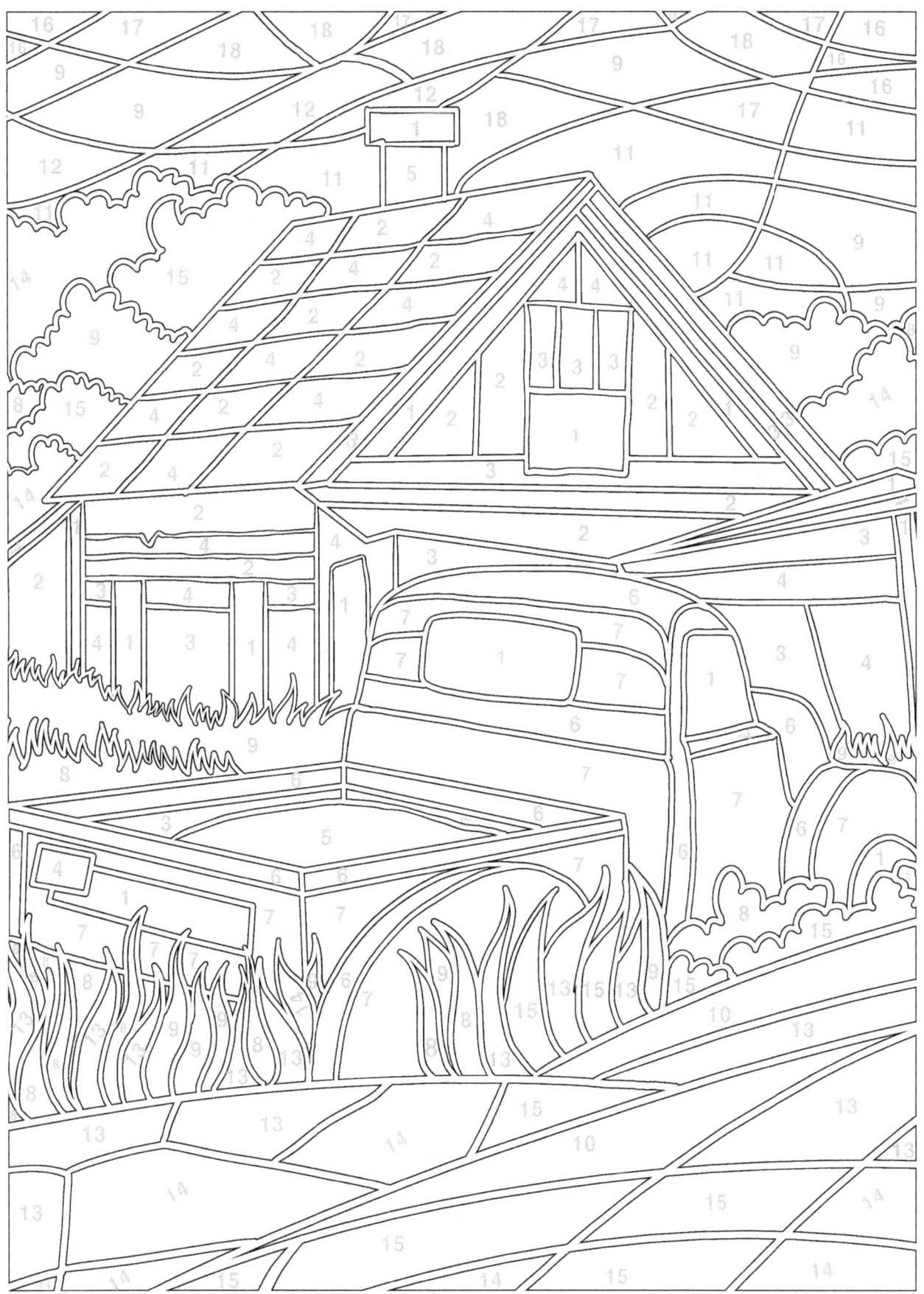

1. Black	16. Light pink
2. Yellow	17. Light Purple
3. Dark Brown	18. Navy Blue
4. Light Brown	20. Orange
5. Gray	
6. Light Gray	
7. Light Orange	
8. Dark Yellow	
9. Light Yellow	
10. Beige	
11. Sky Blue	
12. Medium Blue	
13. Light Green	
14. Medium Green	
15. Dark Green	

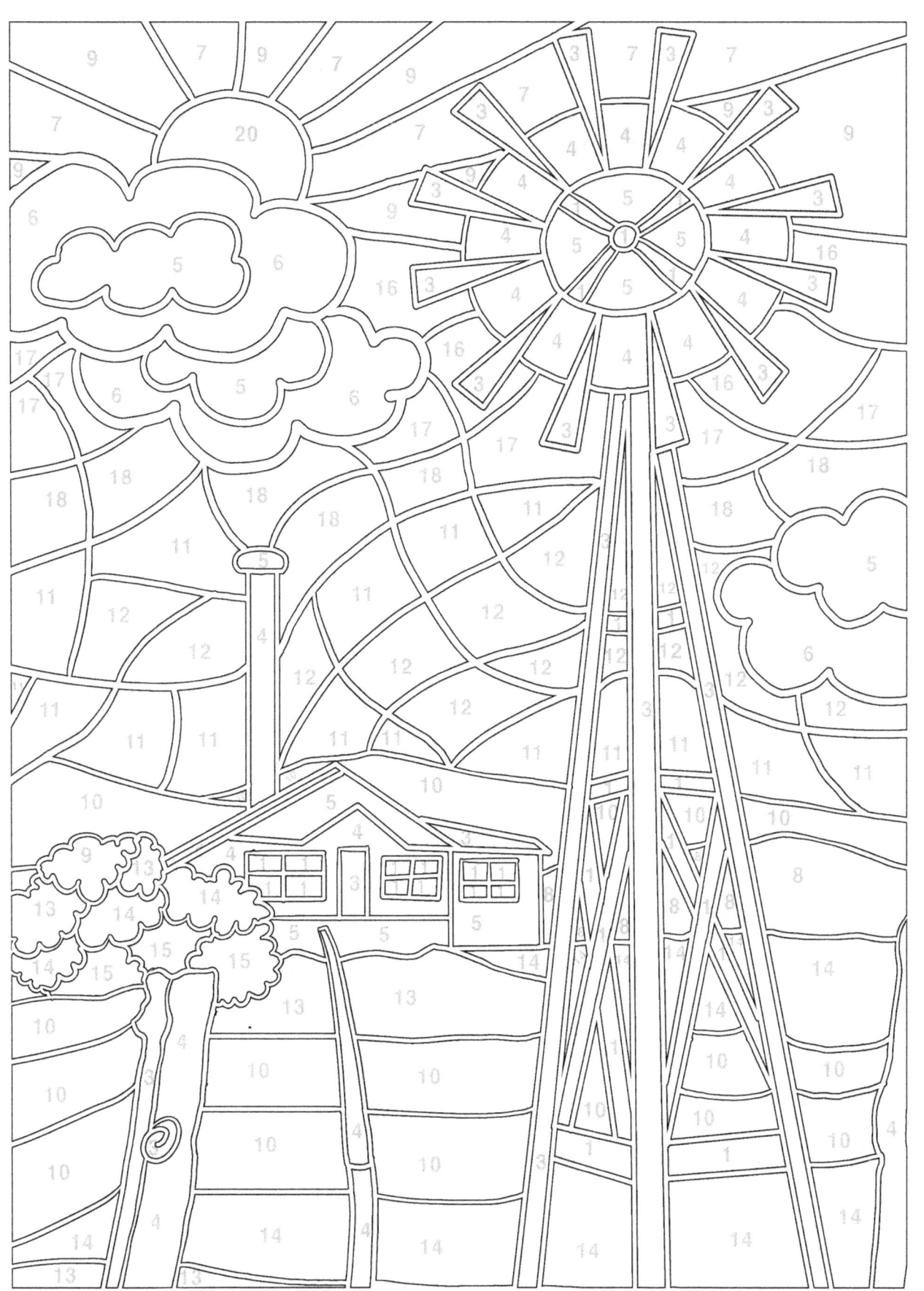

1. Black
2. Reddish Brown
3. Dark Brown
4. Light Brown
5. Golden Yellow
6. Yellow Ocher
7. Red
8. Dark Yellow
9. Light Yellow
10. Beige
11. Sky Blue
12. Medium Blue
13. Light Green
14. Medium Green
15. Dark Green
16. Purple
17. Pink
18. Dark Gray
19. Gray
20. Navy Blue

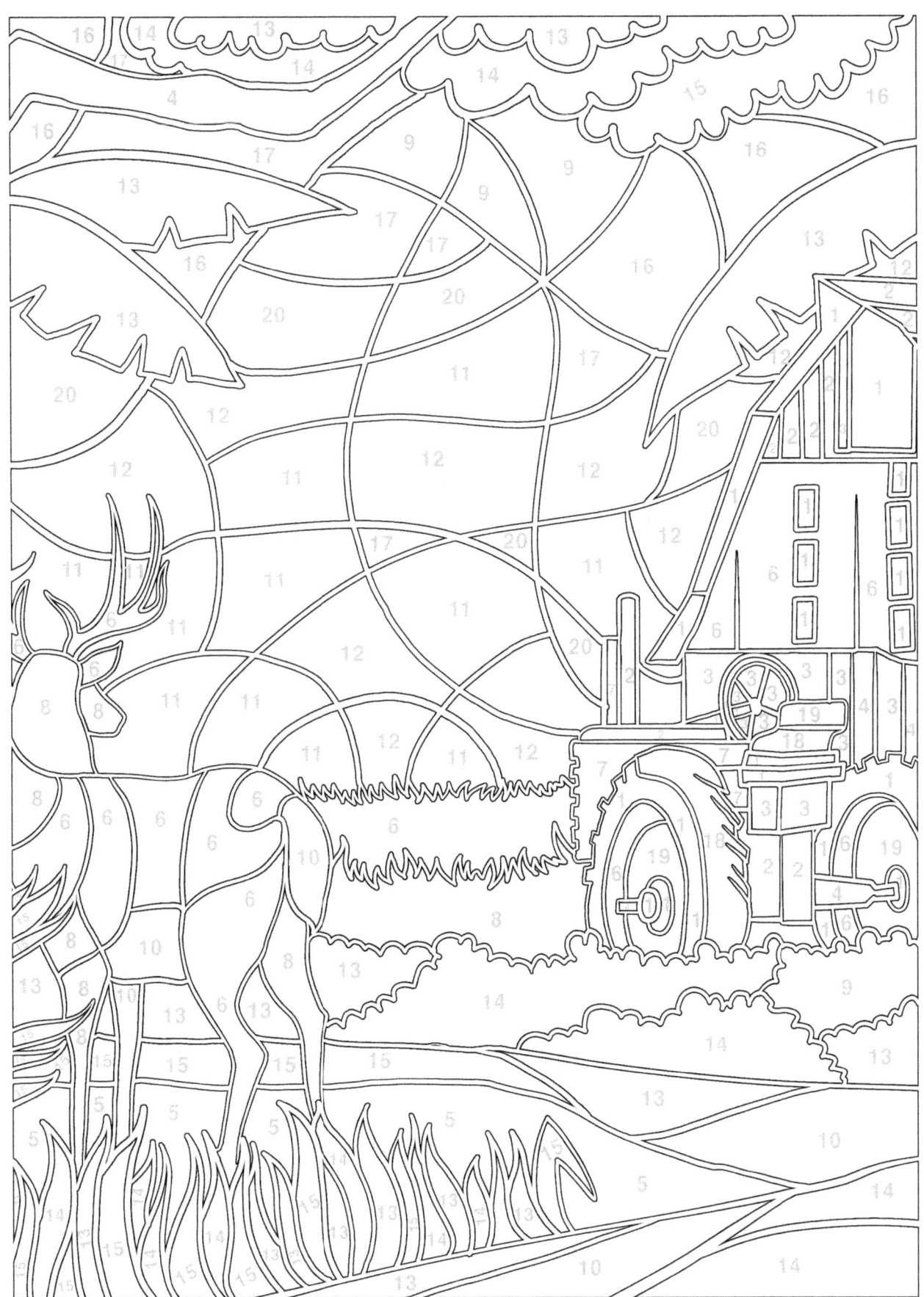

ENJOY BONUS
IMAGES FROM SOME
OF OUR
OTHER FUN
COLOR BY NUMBER
BOOKS!

FIND ALL OF OUR
BOOKS
ON AMAZON

Beautiful Cities and Landmarks
Color by Number
Mosaic World Geography
Coloring Book For Adults

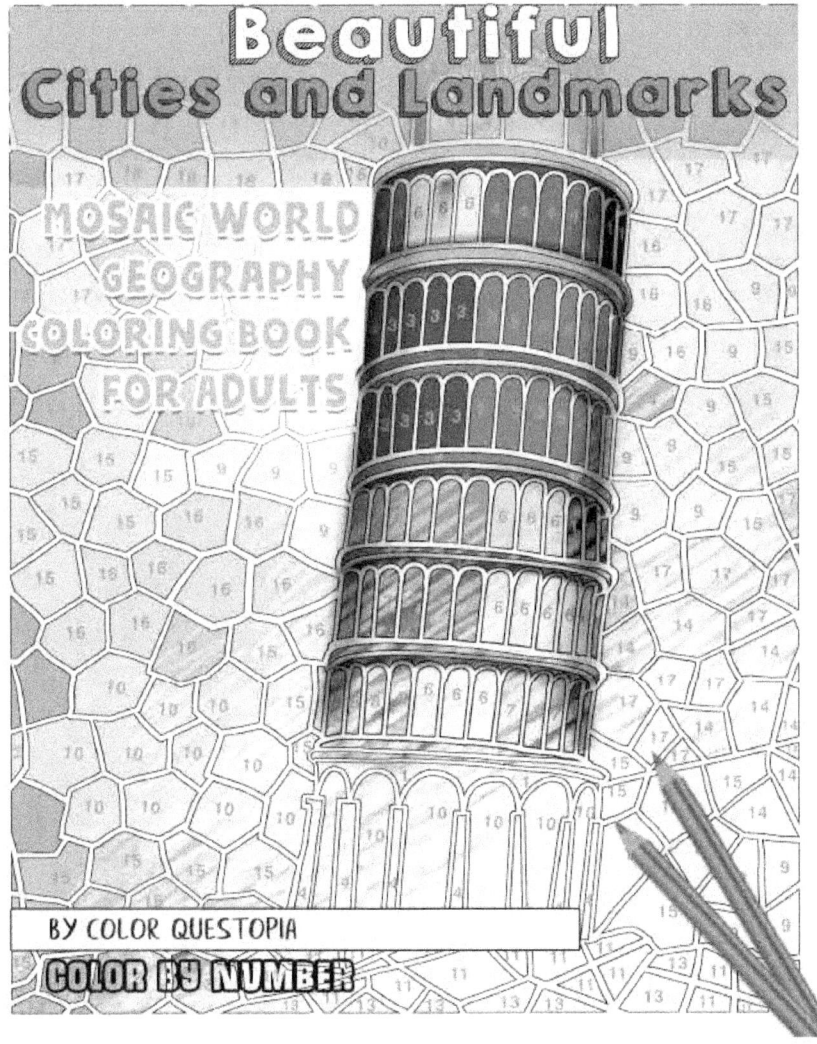

1. Dark Brown
2. Light Red
3. Beige
4. Medium Red
5. Light Yellow
6. Light Green
7. Medium Green
8. Deep Green
9. Orange
10. Army Green
11. Grey Purple
12. Dark Gray
13. Medium Gray
14. Light Gray
15. Gray
16. Light Brown
17. Medium Brown
18. Baby Blue
19. Blue

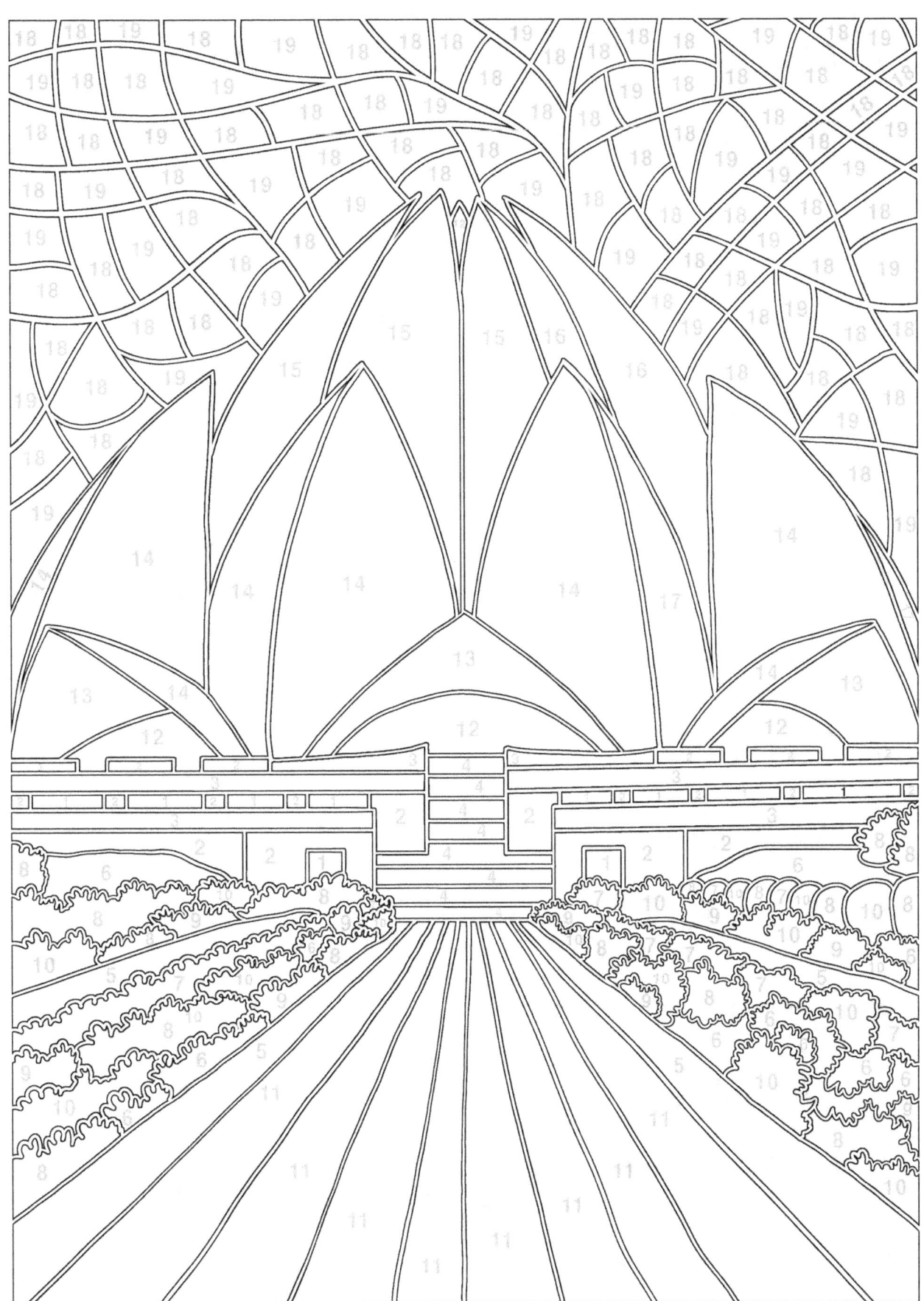

1. Black
2. Iron Gray
3. Dark Brown
4. Gray
5. Medium Gray
6. Beige
7. Sand
8. Slate Gray
9. Ocean Blue
10. Aqua Blue
11. Royal Blue
12. Turquoise Blue
13. Sky Blue
14. Light purple
15. Light Yellow
16. Light pink
17. Pink
18. Medium Blue
19. Pale Turquoise
20. Navy Blue
21. Violet
22. Lemon Yellow

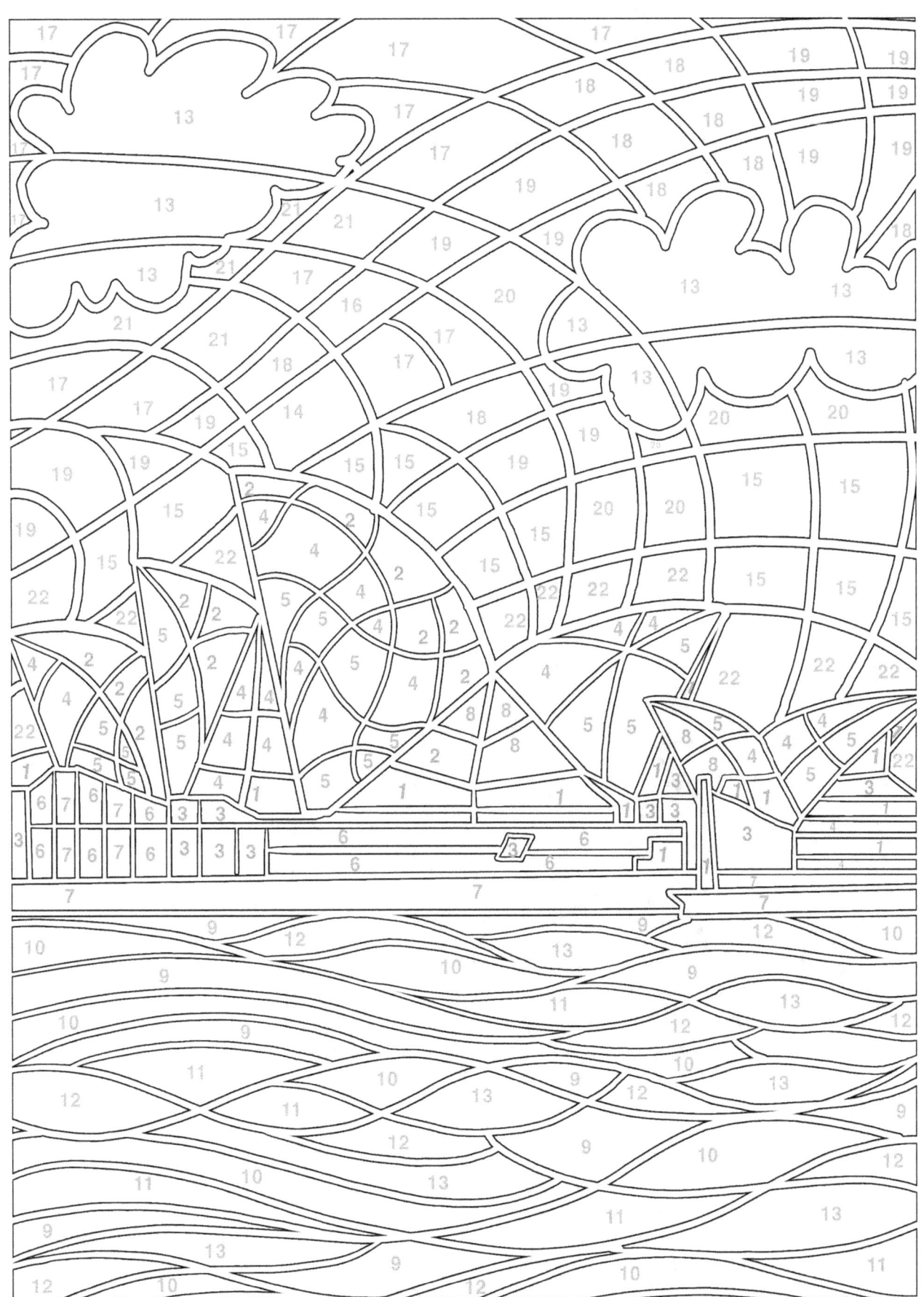

Horses Jumbo Adult Coloring Book
Horses and Ponies Grazing and Racing
Color by Number

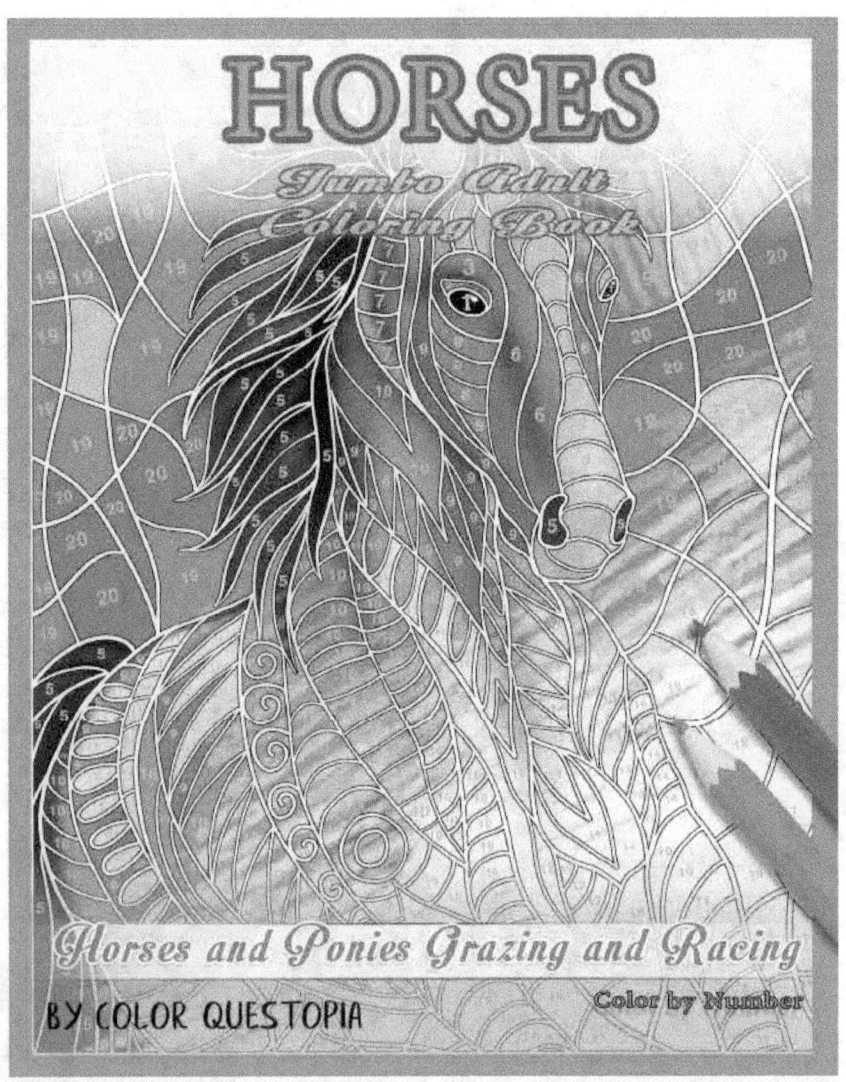

1. Violet

2. Dark violet

3. Soft violet

4. Brown

5. Gray

6. Dark Brown

7. Light Red

8. Pink

9. Light Brown

10. Medium Gray

11. Black

12. Red

13. Medium Green

14. Army green

15. Light green

16. green

17. Dark Green

18. Light Yellow

19. Neon Green

20. White

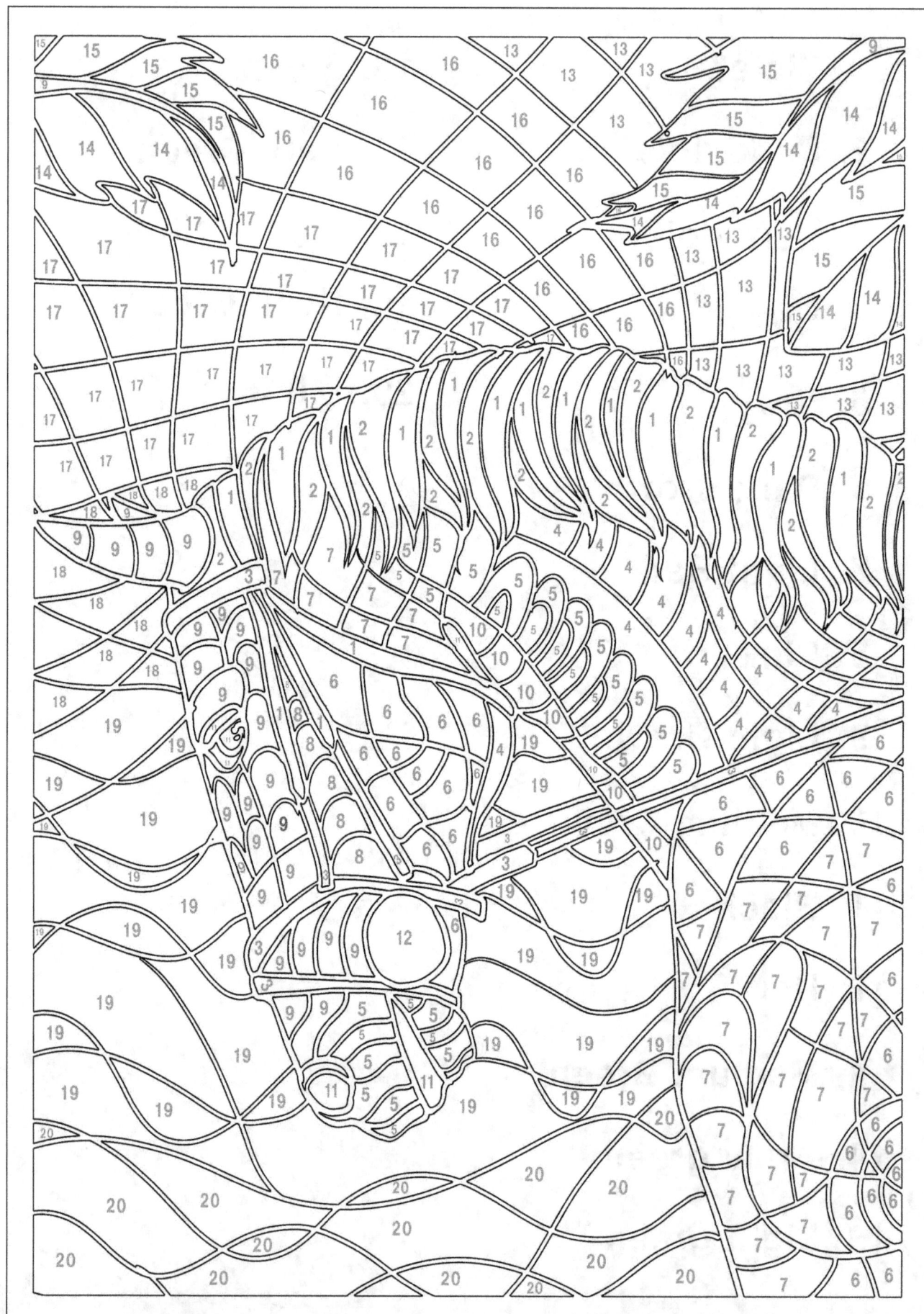

1. Black

2. Brown

3. Dark Brown

4. Light Brown

5. Red

6. Light Yellow

7. Dark Yellow

8. Dark Red

9. Gray

10. Light Gray

11. Medium Purple

12. Soft Violet

13. Dark Blue

14. Medium Green

15. Light Green

16. Deep Green

17. Dark Yellow

18. Yellow

19. Orange

20. Light Orange

21. Pink

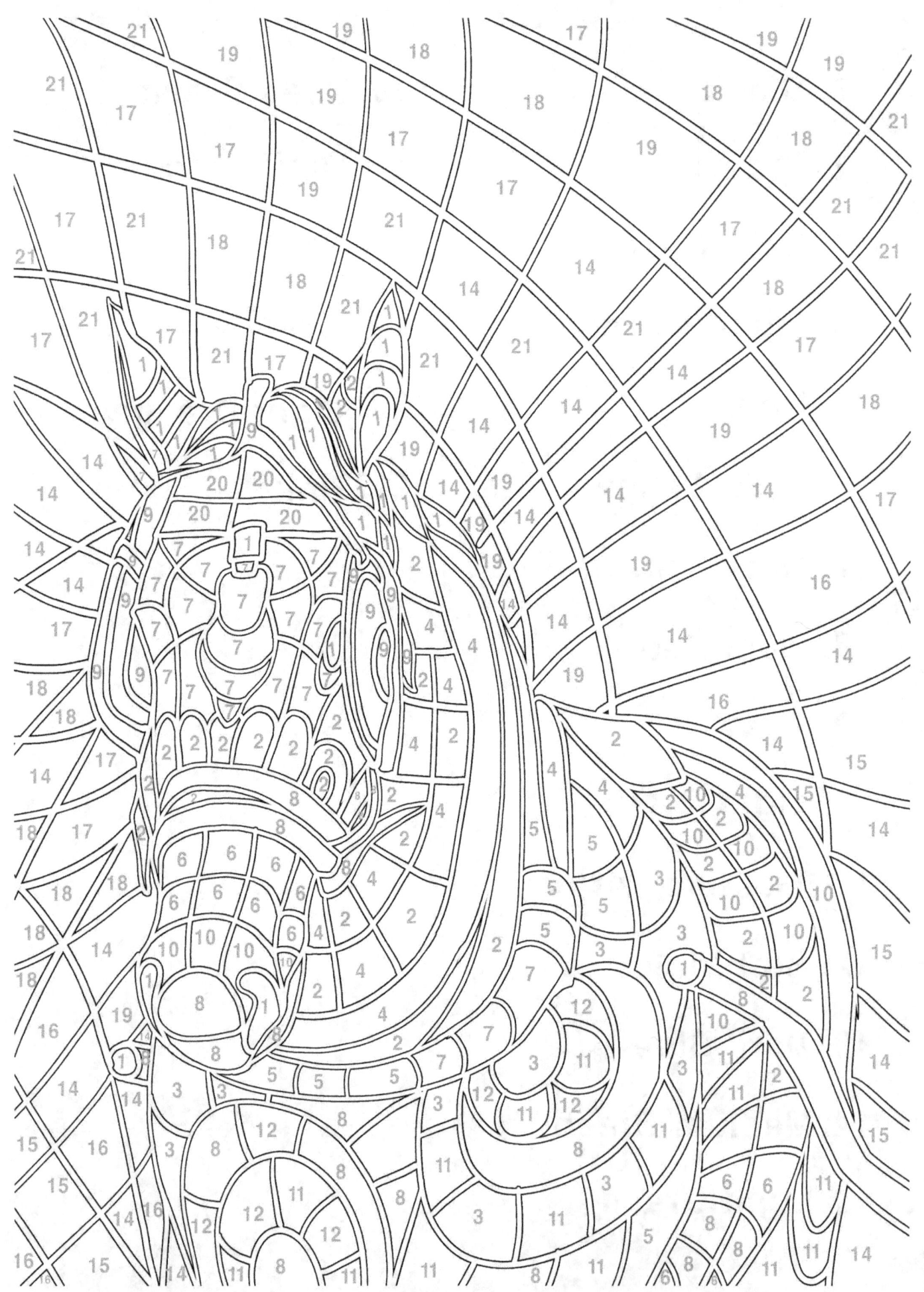

Easy Design
Adult Color By Number
Jumbo Coloring Book of Large Print
Flowers, Birds, and Butterflies

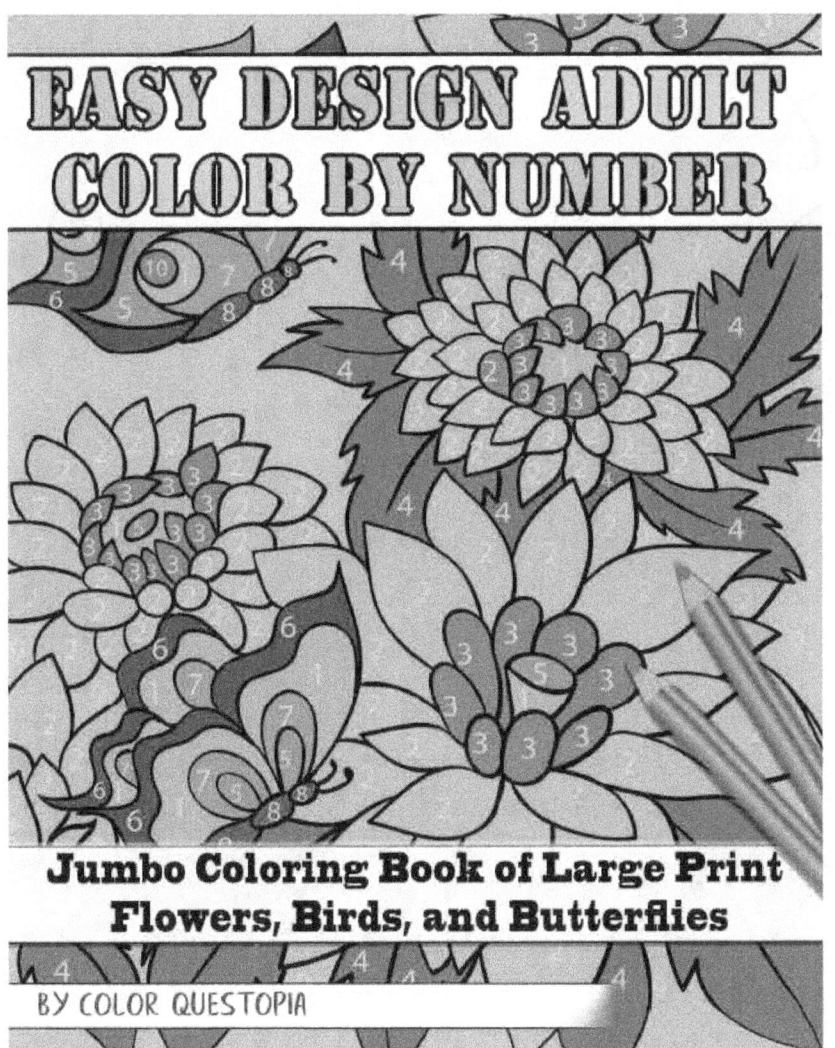

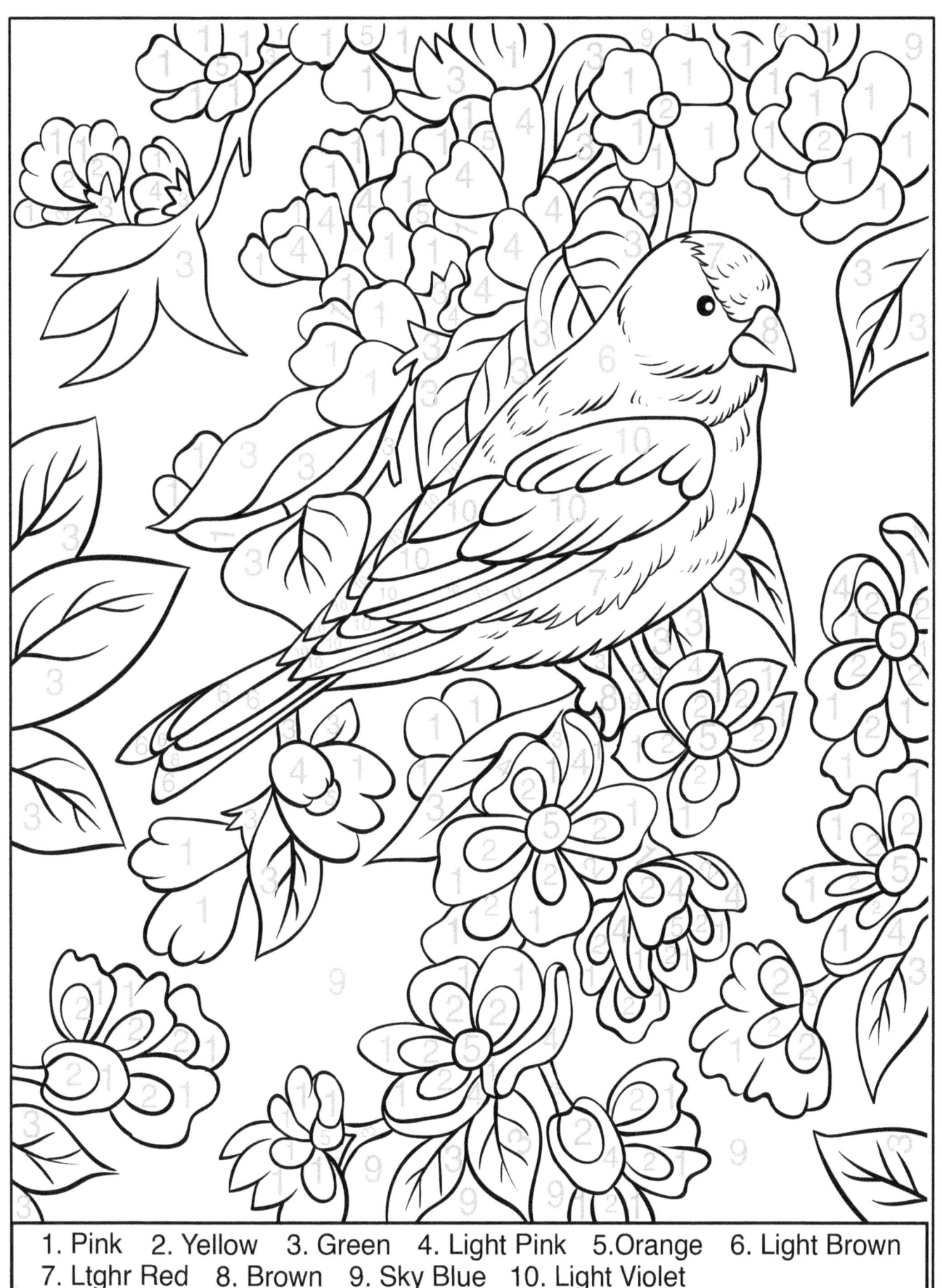

1. Pink   2. Yellow   3. Green   4. Light Pink   5.Orange   6. Light Brown
7. Ltghr Red   8. Brown   9. Sky Blue   10. Light Violet

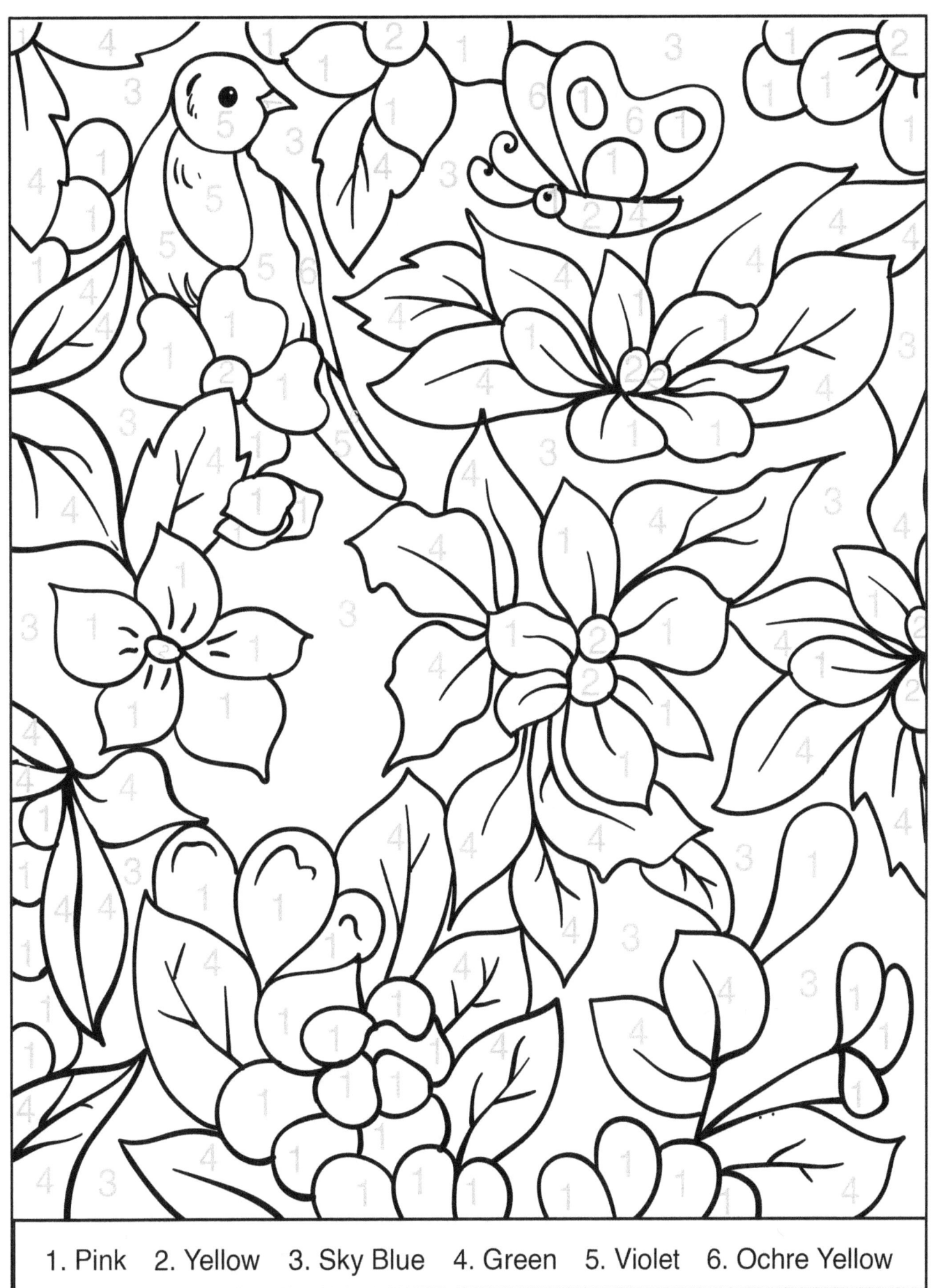

1. Pink   2. Yellow   3. Sky Blue   4. Green   5. Violet   6. Ochre Yellow

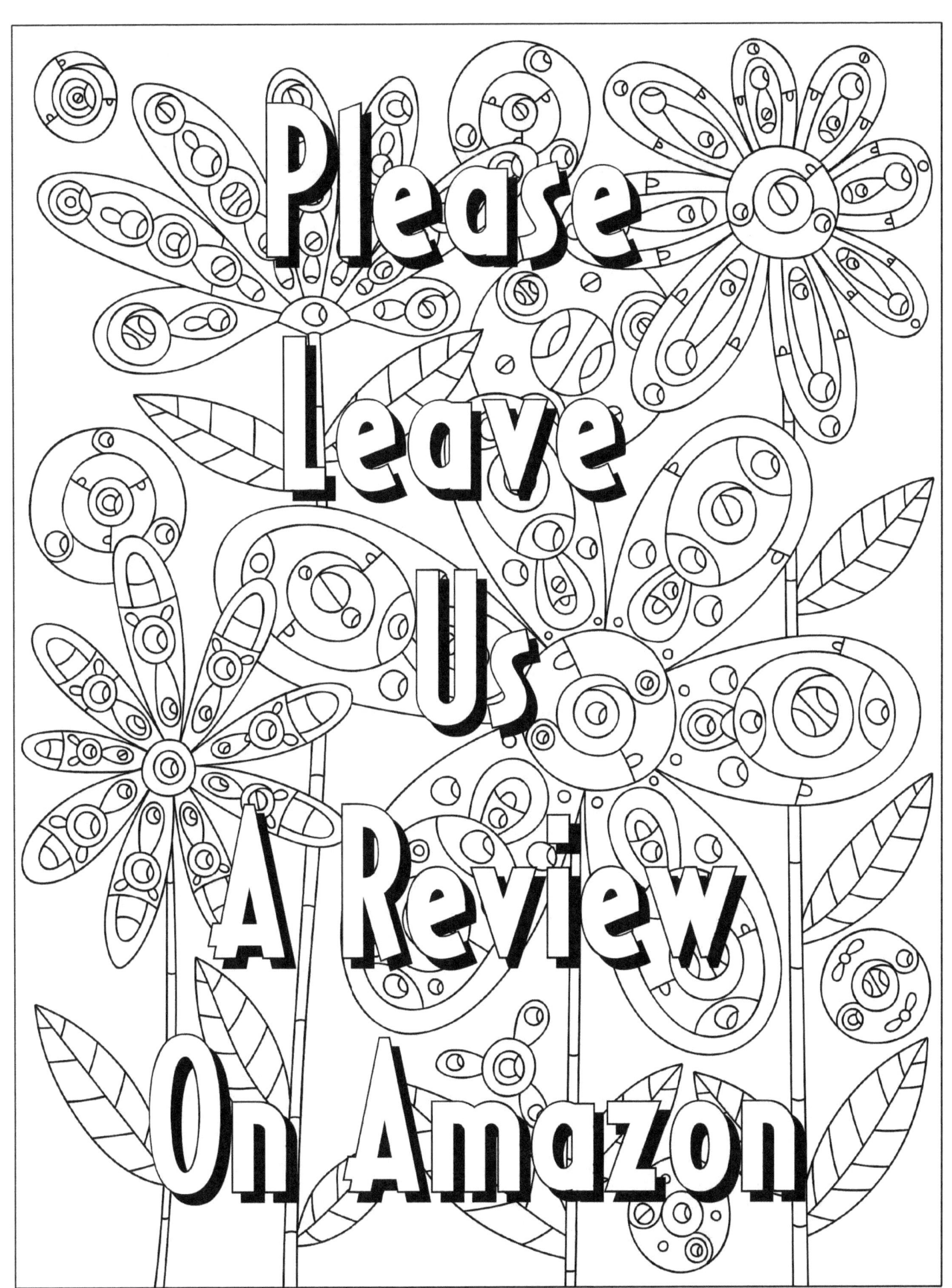